Modelling the Steam Age Railway

Modelling the Steam Age Railway

C. J. Freezer

Patrick Stephens Limited

First published in 1990

British Library Cataloguing in Publication Data
Freezer, C. J. (Cyril John)
  Modelling the steam age railway.
  1. Model steam locomotives.
  Construction
  I. Title
  625.1′9
    ISBN 1–85260–116–7

Patrick Stephens Limited is part of the
Thorsons Publishing Group,
Wellingborough, Northamptonshire
NN8 2RQ, England.

Typeset by Burns & Smith, Derby

Printed in Great Britain at
The Bath Press, Avon

10   9   8   7   6   5   4   3   2   1

Contents

Introduction

Railways are very much a product of the steam age with the result that, even though we have reached the point where few people under 40 have any clear recollection of what it was like to travel behind steam locomotives, the popular image of the railway is still steam-oriented. Nostalgia for a half-forgotten past, when it was always high summer and there was real strawberry jam to spread with the Devonshire clotted cream, is as strong as ever it was. The steam age railway was cast in a heroic mould, it spread its tentacles through every branch of life but it inhabited a totally different world from the one we live in today. If one listens to the men who knew it in its final flowering, one might be inclined to think that something marvellous was rent untimely from our social fabric.

It was nothing of the sort. Steam age railways were wonderful, providing you didn't have to travel on them. At least, if you didn't have to travel on them to get somewhere at a specified time. Always, as a matter of principle, discount the yarns of those of us who travelled on them for their own sake. Steam trains were usually dirty, slow in comparison with their successors and often late.

Railwaymen's reminiscences tend to concentrate of the pleasant aspects of the job. A local footplate trip over a quiet country branch on a warm summer's afternoon, with the small, lightly loaded locomotive in good nick, was about as near paradise as one is likely to encounter in this world. On the other hand, driving a clapped out 'Black Five', with the rear bearings juddering and the big ends loose, a clogged grate, blocked tubes and a tender full of slack was no joke at the best of times — on the Long Drag on a winter's night, with a following gale blowing sleet and coal dust on to the footplate, it was pure purgatory.

Fortunately we can enter the railway room, gently close the door and be in another world. Nostalgia rules, and we are back in a time that really only exists in memory. It can always be summer, there is real ale in the pubs, and the Tudor Cafe serves afternoon teas, with scones, at one shilling and threepence a head. Even Blake's dark satanic mills (and he was, if anything, understating the case) take on a pleasing aspect in 4mm scale. Plastic people don't suffer as did their flesh and blood counterparts.

But, if we are to create the illusion that one is looking at the past, we must get

Left *A 'Hall' Class 4-6-0 heading a train of GW Siphons over Walkham Viaduct, impossible on the prototype, for the loading was too heavy for the lightly built Brunel timber viaduct, but perfectly possible on the Pendon Museum 4mm scale model.*

Far right *Mike Sharman recreates a Bourne engraving with his broad gauge 2-2-2 heading out of a 4mm scale model based closely on the facade of Box tunnel.*

Below right *Stratford St Andrew station on Wally Mayhew's 7mm scale fine-scale layout is typical of a Midland Railway steam age through station.*

things right. Well, I'll modify that — we have to avoid anachronisms for, in presenting a good overall picture, it matters little if some of the models are ever so slightly out of scale, or are not an absolutely faithful copy of the prototype down to the last rivet or cotter-pin. Few people are sufficiently knowledgeable even to recognize the significance of such details. On the other hand, most of us have a fairly good idea when, give or take the odd five years, certain fashions came into being, so a model purporting to represent a pre-group railway before 1914 is ruined if the female figures have skirts that even a lady of the night would not be seen wearing in public. This error, which I have seen in quite advanced circles, is one which, I suggest, the overwhelming majority of the population of Britain could spot at two metres distance. Unfortunately, it is exactly the sort of mistake that is easily made, and as

there are even more traps of this type lying half hidden to snare the uninformed, the whole business of modelling the steam age might be considered fraught with difficulty.

It isn't. The traditional way of gleaning information on the past was to find a garrulous old fellow in a pub, ply him with ale and listen avidly. It was a little chancy, as he was apt to embroider his stories. You could also turn to the historian. This is not altogether a good thing, as historians tend, alas, to get bogged down with irrelevant detail. One can hardly blame them — if you were to spend a goodly slice of your life sifting through musty archives, you'd be anxious to show something for all your efforts.

In this book I hope to provide a clear guide to the basic shape and form of the British steam age railway as it can be applied by an individual modeller within the restrictions of his own home. I feel I can do this with some authority. For a start, not only was I born in 1924, but, for the first 15 years of my life, we had a railway at the end of the garden. Ever since my teens I've clambered over, cycled around, travelled on and visited railway lines by car. I have amassed a fairly large library, I've not only spoken to old railwaymen, but I've also known older enthusiasts who told me how things were before I was born. I also have a very clear memory and can recall the mechanics of a way of life that, thankfully, no longer exists in this country. Furthermore I served an apprenticeship in steam engineering and have a sound grounding in the workshop practice of the steam age.

Whilst it has proved impractical, as I knew at the outset, to cram the essence

of several thousand books and the experience of a lifetime into one volume, I trust I have covered the field sufficiently to give any keen modeller a head start. It has been necessary to omit several desirable things — there is no room for narrow gauge and I have had to confine myself to British prototypes. Worse, there is not room for even a brief bibliography. I console myself with the thought that I have not had to make an invidious choice between authors!

C. J. Freezer
Hemel Hempstead

Key to plans

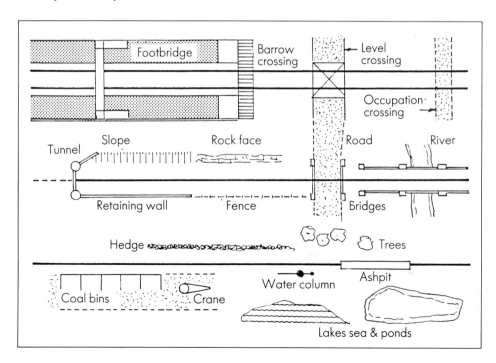

CHAPTER 1
The historic viewpoint

The steam age on Britain's railways extended from 1830 to 1960. Of course, steam locomotives were in use in the 1820s, but until the Liverpool & Manchester Railway was built most railways that were around relied on horse traction and supplemented this with stationary engines. Indeed, the whole purpose of the Rainhill Trials was to find out if a locomotive engine could pull a train at a reasonable speed from Liverpool to Manchester without breaking down *en route*. Up to then, there were good grounds for doubting the machine's reliability and commercial future.

Steam was also still in evidence until the late 1960s, but by then the effects of the Beeching-inspired vandalism had so transformed the scene that there was little left of the steam age railway that I, and so many others, knew and loved. Although we have preserved lines, and steam specials, they are not the same thing, and to recreate the ambience of the steam age it is necessary to make a model.

A steam age model is an historical record — up to a point. I'd like to stress this, since many authoritative writers have placed so much emphasis on this aspect of modelling as to create what is,

in my opinion, a serious imbalance. In particular, I must criticize most severely the idea that any model must be absolutely accurate, *lest it mislead some future historian.*

Poppycock! A historian, as opposed to a mere antiquary, is well aware that all humans are fallible, and indeed history has been defined as the record of mankind's inevitable cock-ups. A historian knows that any source is unreliable unless cross-checked, for even where the writer was not lying in his teeth for a reason that seemed good at the time, he may have been labouring under an honest misconception. Just compare any two newspapers' accounts of the same event, ideally one you attended yourself. As for the much vaunted official records, well, in my opinion, Disraeli got it wrong — the third and ultimate category of falsehood is not statistics, but general arrangement drawings.

More to the point, modelling should be a fun thing. It isn't necessary to have everything 100 per cent correct — anything over a generous 60 per cent is fairly good, something in excess of 80 per cent is marvellous. I am, in particular, thinking not so much of in-

Above *Hornby produced this 4mm scale model of* Rocket *in its Rainhill Trials condition and added a pleasing model of the replica Liverpool & Manchester first class coach to complete the set. As* Rocket *was extensively modified and repainted before going into service, this train, whilst satisfying to the eye, is technically incorrect.*

Below *One of Mike Sharman's mid-Victorian stations. Although all his models are closely based on actual prototypes, they came from different railways and would never have been seen together in reality. This did not detract one iota from the charm of the layout.*

dividual models of odd incidental details, such as locomotives, coaches and similar accessories in the overall scene, but the model railway as a single coherent whole. Indeed, I recognize three quite distinct themes in historical modelling.

The first is nostalgic modelling, where the intention is to highlight features the modeller considers of interest. An excellent example of this genre was the late Cyril Fry's Irish International Railway. This 7mm scale model contained examples of locomotives which ran on Irish metals, to broad, narrow and no gauge at all, each heading a typical train of its period. Antique 2–2–2s ran alongside models of the CIE's earlier diesels and Bulleid's abortive turf-burning beastie, regardless of the fact that geographically and in time they never came together.

The second category is the imagined prototype. Peter Denny's 'Buckingham' and Frank Dyer's 'Borchester' are excellent examples of this style of model. The railways are fictional — Frank's layout even serves a fictional location — but although Peter's model appears to serve actual localities, they could only exist in an alternative universe, for the model 'Buckingham' is a large, bustling cathedral city. The important point about both models is that not only do they visually recreate their locale and time-slot, in one case the Great Central Railway in the Edwardian era, in the other the Eastern Region of British Railways in the final years of steam, but also the lines are operated exactly as the prototype might have been, with correct signalling and a proper timetable.

The final category is prototypical modelling. Here an actual station is lovingly recreated. Again I cite two examples, Alan William's 'Aylesbury' and Stan Robert's 'Bakewell'. They differ slightly, since the second 'Aylesbury' makes few, if any, compromises, whereas 'Bakewell' was cunningly compressed to fit into a relatively small room. It is as well to point out that, in the popular 4mm scale, few prototype stations scale anything under 7m, while many require more than 10m if they are to be faithfully reproduced to exact scale. Even in 2mm scale, compromise is often required. The MRC's 'Chiltern Green' and 'Luton Hoo', now at Oakwood Manor near Bath, models both stations with reasonable accuracy, since they're very simple prototypes, but not only plays havoc with the distance between them, but has a few other freelance touches as well. I only know this because I was told it was so — it isn't easy to tell where the compromises were made.

The point I want to make is not only that there are these three perfectly valid approaches, but also that there is absolutely no way anyone can say that one is better than another, because, demonstrably, each approach has produced a model that is not only satisfying to the builder — the main object of the exercise — but has captured the imagination of thousands of enthusiasts as well. There is, alas, a strong tendency in some quarters to lay down rigid rules and regulations defining a good or a bad model. I prefer a simpler approach — does the model give its owner pleasure?

The steam age lasted for 130 years. Clearly, the only way one can depict the entire sweep of the period is by the nostalgic theme, where a model *Rocket* can share tracks with a Stanier streamlined 'Pacific'. Otherwise one has to beware of anachronisms and geo-

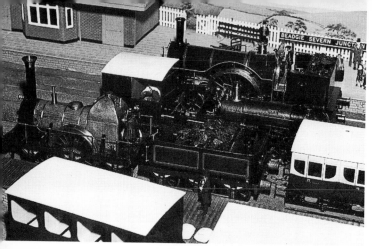

Left *Broad gauge to the fore! GWR 2-2-2* Actaeon *heading over a low timber viaduct on Bill Salter's 7mm scale period model railway, and also in the company of South Devon 0-4-0* Owl *and a Bristol & Exeter 4-2-4 tank.*

Below right *A 4mm scale Stephenson 0-4-2 on the Bolton Club's 1830s 4mm scale layout. The buildings are stark and new, a mute reminder that they were brand new at the model's period. An early cattle truck is the first wagon in the train.*

graphical inconsistencies. Ideally, it would be pleasant to have every individual model on the layout representative of its prototype at one very precise moment in time. Unfortunately, this just isn't possible because when we set out to make a reasonably faithful model of anything, we need some accurate references to tell us how it looked, and for this we have to rely on authenticated drawings and photographs, used in conjunction with one another. Unfortunately things get altered, and even where we're able to collect a reasonable selec-

tion of illustrations, we can find that there are discrepancies. For this reason, whilst it may appear desirable to fix a target date — say 27 June 1924 — we should allow a tolerance of several years on either side and be prepared to move our target if either the weight of evidence falls to one side, or, more likely, we discover that some very desirable feature we simply must include was either scrapped or wasn't built at our target date. Furthermore, before 1930 the time band ought to be something like five years, whilst should you wish to move before 1890, you will find it extremely difficult to be as precise as this, simply because the records begin to get patchy.

The point you must bear in mind is that in order to build a model, it is not enough to know that the prototype existed — you also have to know how it looked. It's not too difficult to lay your hands on accurate locomotive registers, even for the most obscure of minor railways. The problem is that all too often in the early years, the appearance of many of these machines is a matter for conjecture. On occasions, all that is known is that there is a record in an old manuscript list which suggests that a particular locomotive was owned by a particular company. When one turns to coaches and wagons, there is even less information to be had. Track layouts of early stations are equally vague, though it has to be said that there is a fair amount of information available on the earliest lines, and the GWR broad gauge is reasonably well covered, largely because it was so controversial.

Nonetheless, from 1890 until 1960, the British railway scene appeared unchanging and immutable. Yes, there were new and larger locomotives, new

longer and wider coaches and the colours changed from time to time, but by and large things were much as they always were. The differences, whilst very significant to the railway enthusiast, passed over the heads of the great majority of travellers. Even the timetables seemed much the same; indeed, with a few odd exceptions, the trains of the 1950s had their close counterparts in the 1900s.

After 1960, diesels appeared, branches closed and complete routes vanished, leading to the present-day railway scene which, whilst equally fascinating, is not germane to this book. Before 1890, not only does information become extremely patchy, but there is little support in the way of kits. However, providing you are prepared to invest in a good library, it is feasible to scratchbuild a mid-Victorian railway, whilst modelling the early days of the Liverpool & Manchester or the Stockton & Darlington is a perfectly practical proposition.

But it is the 1950s that is the most popular period for railway modellers; it is the one best served by complete models and kits and will be the period considered in this book.

Above Carlisle, *the Bishop's Castle Railway 0–6–0 taken about 1900, with various members of staff obscuring the detail. This is an annoying feature of many old locomotive photographs.*

Below *The explanation of the intrusive figures. When the BBC was filming its version of* The Hound of the Baskervilles *at Staverton Bridge on the Dart Valley railway, several members of the DVRA Committee were roped in as extras. I was asked to photograph the group, and without thinking I said, 'OK, all stand in front of the engine'! It wasn't until the photo was developed that I realized I'd followed an ancient tradition.*

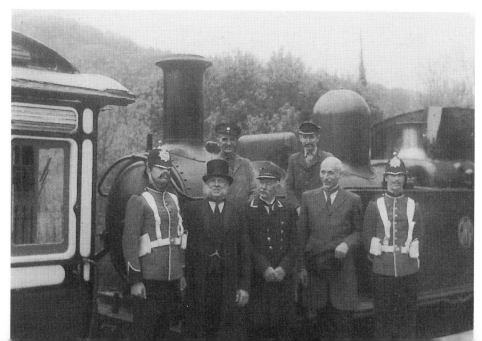

CHAPTER 2
Research is redundant

Because all steam age models are, by definition, historical, you are likely to be told that 'Research must come first'. However, one of the finest historical model railways, Peter Denny's 'Buckingham', was built without any research at all. I have this on the best possible authority, Peter Denny himself. At this point, I ought to make one important observation, which is that reading a textbook is most definitely not research, nor is finding a drawing — the research involved in both was done by someone else. That it does take a little while to look out all the references to a particular prototype goes without saying, but it's surprising just how much information can be discovered in a couple of hours in a well stocked library.

However, let us revert to Peter Denny's method, which is one I would heartily recommend; just consider the results! At the outset he knew that the Great Central Railway existed, and a quick check on the Skinley blueprint catalogue revealed that there were enough drawings available to produce a limited selection of Great Central models. As everything had to be scratchbuilt in those days, this apparently meagre amount of information

provided work for a couple of years, by which time some more information had been found. And so it went on, with information turning up rather faster than even a dedicated modeller like Peter Denny could apply it.

That was some 40 years ago. Today, the situation is rather different. I am writing this book in my den, a small, cosy room lined with books. I can, in a matter of minutes, lay my hands on detailed information on some fairly obscure prototypes, whilst so far as my abiding love, the Great Western, is concerned, there are scores of books covering virtually every aspect of the railway. There is information on dozens of prototypes, and in some cases virtually all one needs to know to begin an effective model is given either in a readily obtainable book or a recent magazine article. At the outset you are not likely to have an extensive railway library, and it took me decades to make my own collection. You may have better things to do with the space, and far better things to do with the money. There are other ways of going about it.

Your local public library can, in theory, obtain a copy of virtually any book published since the war. This is fine, if you know which books you want and are prepared to pay for the service. Alternatively, you can make use of a specialized library. The Historical Model Railway Society, which exists to help anyone modelling our railway past, has a very extensive library. It is kept at the Model Railway Club's headquarters in Islington, and since the MRC itself also has an extensive library, there are few books of any use to a railway modeller that cannot be consulted on the Thursday evenings when the MRC has its track nights. Furthermore, for those members unable to visit London, there is a photocopying service, and since there are many knowledgeable members on hand on any club night, it isn't difficult to track down references to any specific fact. Of course, if you've selected a particularly obscure prototype, you may have problems, but in this context obscure means something owned by a minor railway before 1900.

Of course, you won't find out everything about a chosen railway, but it isn't necessary. A model railway is quite unlike any other type of model, as it is not so much a single model but a collection of congruous models which go to make up the complete layout. The locomotives, coaches and wagons which, for most of us, are the main feature of the layout, are by their very nature detachable and hence readily changed. The buildings, whilst more firmly attached to the modelled landscape, are still easily removed and replaced. Only the track itself is in any way a fixture. But even the permanent way itself can be altered if need be, but as steam age track layouts are not dated, or even tied to any one company, there's little need to modify this part of the model in order to improve its

Alton Towers, on the North Staffordshire Railway, was a simple through station notable for its elaborate station buildings, constructed to blend with the nearby house, now the centre of a modern theme park. The station, alas, is no more.

historical accuracy.

Obviously, before beginning any individual part of the model railway, it's a good idea to find out just what it looked like. If you're making up a kit, or adding detail to a commercial model, you'll find that a few photographs and a scale drawing, assuming one isn't included in the kit, could be useful. If you're scratch-building, then a scale drawing and photographs will be essential. However, unless you happen to have decided on so obscure a prototype that no information whatever exists in any readily available source, you won't be doing

---

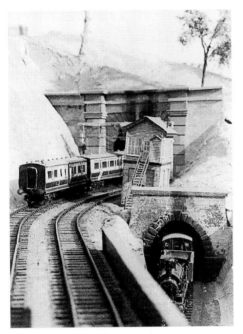

A corner of Jack Nelson's first HO gauge LNWR layout, built in the 1950s and one of the earliest layouts to be based firmly on detailed research. As Jack put all his researches into an excellent, fully illustrated book, and others have added more detail, there is no need to undertake fresh research to construct a model of this calibre.

any research. You'll find a lot of the information you need in books and magazines.

Research can be very counterproductive. For a start, never forget that it not only interferes with modelmaking, it also puts a stop to operation as well. It is extremely seductive, and every fact unearthed seems to point the way to a dozen more. Each time one thinks one is finally getting to the end of a trail, what appears to be the final piece of data serves to destroy the comfortable

hypothesis you have established. Indeed, I've often felt that research is rather like building a house of cards — all too often the final result is a mess.

Worse, there is no guarantee of success. The most elementary facts have a habit of being utterly elusive. To take a concrete example, my old friend Jack Nelson spent a lifetime studying the LNWR and in *LNWR Portrayed* presented a wealth of detailed information on the railway, accurately aligned to the modeller. Unfortunately, he was not able to track down a single contemporary reference to the colours of the station buildings and, whilst one could deduce that they were probably light and dark stone, and nearly identical to the LMS hues, this lacked absolute certainty.

Some while later, whilst reviewing Hamilton Ellis' *Railway Art*, my eye was caught by a Tissot painting, showing a young lady of fashion standing on the up slow platform at Willesden Junction sometime in the 1880s. She was clearly alone and had an expression compounded of boredom, annoyance and disdain, understandable in the circumstances. I am certain she has just discovered that the positive advice she had from her brother is all wrong and that her own idea, that she should have gone to Euston instead, was correct.

It was then that I realized that here was the detail Jack had been seeking, for the artist's rendering of the station and the North London train in the background was so accurate that he had clearly been on site and made a series of colour sketches for his composition. As a matter of interest, the colours were, after all, those used by the LMS, give or take a shade. At last, the final nail had been driven in, but it was not through

Princetown (GWR) in the 1930s, a photograph in the author's collection taken by S.R. Loxton, an early proponent of prototype station research. Regrettably only a few of his negatives have survived.

detailed research, but the action of blind chance.

The point is that had Jack waited until he had this confirmation before building any models, he wouldn't have built a single item. Unfortunately, there are cases where modellers are falling into this trap. This error is compounded by the knowledge that a good deal of the essential information was recorded at one time. The danger lies in assuming that it still exists.

It is known that the GWR had an almost obsessive passion for photography and, moreover, retained most of its negatives. It is also known that the Southern threw a lot away and that the Midland lost many valuable records in a fire. However, back to the GWR.

Photos exist of a whole range of unlikely items, the more interesting of which have been published in sumptuous volumes over the past couple of decades. It is unsafe to assume from this that a photograph therefore exists of every individual item. It may well have been taken, though there is no conclusive way of proving this. It may well have been destroyed as being of little interest.

There is, for example, the case of the mysterious No 9, a GWR 4-2-4 standard gauge tank locomotive which was definitely built but which Swindon wished had never got off the drawing board. The story is that it fell off the track at every other turnout on its one and only run in steam. It was then hidden under tarpaulins, and finally some parts were used to make a reliable 2-2-2. No photo exists, nor are there drawings in the archives, and there is only one conjectural reconstruction. Whether the machine got as far as the photo site is open to question, but it is certain that had a photograph been taken, the fragile glass negative was dropped, accidentally on purpose.

Apart from this, records do get lost. Several of my own negatives have gone missing, and when, some years ago, I received the railway notes of S.R. Loxton, one of the pioneers of prototype station study, I was saddened to discover that only about 10 per cent of the negatives had survived. I could multiply these instances time and time again. The simple fact is that there is not enough space and certainly not enough time to save everything and, more important still, to so record and annotate every item that someone else can locate it without too much difficulty. Research follows a hyperbolic curve; the initial information is fairly easy to locate, but when you get to around 70 per cent of your information needs, difficulties begin and it takes roughly twice as much time and effort to get from 70 per cent information to 85 per cent as it did to get from zero to 70 per cent. After 85 per cent, the going gets very hard.

There is one simple solution to research. Take the best information you can find and from this build the very best model you can and place the result on exhibition. If we ignore the real difficulties involved in making a good model, this is a straightforward business, and Murphy's law states that if there is an error in your prototype information, the one individual who has that missing detail will see the model and tell you where you went wrong. You then build the definitive model. This is much quicker and far less trouble than hunting for the information yourself.

Above all, remember that the best excuse for not having built a model is 'my researches are not yet complete'. The fact is, they never will be!

Above *Mortehoe station, Southern Railway, in the 1930s. Another of S.R. Loxton's record photographs, it shows a simple through station. On the left, the signal box is sandwiched between the original LSWR station buildings and a Southern Railway concrete store shed.*

Below *Kingswear, GWR, in 1949. A 'Hall' is waiting to leave, and immediately behind is a 'Dreadnaught' coach of the early 1900s, built to the GWR's full loading gauge, the doors being recessed to give greater room to open. The three vans beyond are interesting; the nearest is a four-wheel Southern Utility, the furthest an LMS full brake. The central vehicle is a GWR Fruit D.*

CHAPTER 3
The steam age layout

A model railway consists of two distinct parts, the layout itself and the rolling-stock. Despite the obvious attraction of the steam locomotive, it is the layout that is the real key to an effective steam age model. Moreover, it represents the largest single modelling project and, although it is in itself made up from a number of individual models linked by the tracks and the associated landscape, it has to be considered as a whole during the planning and construction stages.

There is another, more significant feature. There is no fundamental difficulty in making a true-to-scale model of a locomotive, coach or wagon to any of the accepted modelling scales. There is a very serious bar to the construction of a true-to-scale model of a station — its size. Only in 2mm scale is it feasible to model a station to scale in the sort of space likely to be found in the normal home, and even here the choice is limited to the simpler prototypes.

I am well aware that there were many steam age stations which, for one reason or another, were extremely compact and thus capable of being modelled, to scale, in quite small areas. Unfortunately, they were also very limited in their scope, and operationally, very little happened at the station. As a pure modelling project, such a model has charm, but it also has built-in obsolescence.

To a certain extent, the space problem can be circumvented by a group project, but even so, to suggest that in order to enjoy the best of the hobby you must either be very well-to-do or have to sink your individuality into a club project is, to me, anathema. It not only reeks of elitism, it is also self-defeating. The wide range of ready-to-run models, kits and detailed components available today has come about because the hobby is broadly based on the privately owned layout. Or, to use a phrase closely associated with a magazine I edited for a good many years, on the existence of the average enthusiast. Over the years I've had a good deal of criticism, some of it vituperative, from individuals who believe that any deviation from their self-imposed parameters is a heinous crime worthy of immersion in boiling oil. I could answer in a like vein, but I prefer Mark Twain's aphorism: 'God must like ordinary people, he makes so many of them'.

Fortunately it isn't essential to model a station precisely to scale. Very few people know just how big a full-size station

can be, for we normally view the prototype from ground level and the distances are foreshortened. It is possible to reduce distances by as much as 50 per cent without it being too obvious, and many apparently accurate layouts are, in fact, well under scale. One common error lies in believing that country branch stations are smaller in area than their main-line equivalents, whereas in fact many city termini were more compact. Country branch stations are simpler and, because train lengths are shorter, are more amenable to drastic, but proportional, reduction. As always, an advantage must be traded against a snag — it is a trifle difficult to account for the appearance of large express locomotives and rakes of main-line

coaches at the end of a rural branch. As a result, one loses the very part of the steam age railway that created its enduring appeal. The 'Irish Mail', 'Flying Scotsman', 'Cornish Riviera Express' and 'Bournemouth Belle' are part and parcel of the glamour of steam, but you can't run them down a branch!

However, before I deal with the details, there is an important general principle to consider. Most of the smaller branches and many secondary routes which formed a significant part of the steam age have vanished forever, leaving no more than the disused trackbed behind, if that. This is hardly news to any reader. What is less obvious is that, in the quarter century since steam disappeared, the physical appearance of

Above left *Heathfield station, GWR, in 1949, looking towards Moretonhampstead. This junction on a quiet branch line had no footbridge – passengers had to walk the length of the down platform and use the barrow crossing. The Exe Valley line curves to the right beyond the platform end. Note that this is a full double junction even though both lines were single track branches. The line to the left runs into a factory and remained in use long after the modern dual carriageway that now crosses the site was built.*

Left *St Annes Park, Bristol, in the late '60s. The cutting resulted from a widening of one of the original tunnels to allow additional goods lines to be laid in. Note the rare case of a steam-age ladder crossover connection; this was permissible since it was not used for passenger traffic.*

Right *The down end of Honiton, Southern Region, in April 1957. Note the variation in platform levels and style.*

what is left has also changed. I am not so much thinking of such superficial matters as the new station colours and modern signboards that abound today; there are more fundamental differences arising from the complete elimination of less-than-wagon-load traffic, the complete change in domestic fuel usage, the abandonment of livestock traffic and many other features of the steam age railway. Track layouts have been radically altered. Not only have the old-pattern small goods yards become car parks or industrial estates, but several fundamental changes in practice have also come about. Of these, the main one is the arrangement of junctions, for in place of the present-day ladder connections there were double junctions, even where the branch was single track.

In addition, many structures that were required for the old-style working have either been demolished or converted to other uses with a concomitant change in appearance. Station buildings have been modernized (not before time in many cases), with the result that it is no longer possible to do as so many of us did in my youth — walk down to the nearest bit of railway line and take notes.

In the following chapters I shall be describing the arrangement of steam age stations and auxiliary features of the railway, not from the strict prototype angle, but from the way one may reproduce them in miniature within the normal home. In every case, I shall be assuming 4mm scale is being followed, partly for consistency but mainly because it is the predominant size in use at present and offers the largest choice for the steam age modeller, a subject I will explore in more detail in later chapters.

Avonmouth station, GWR, in the early '50s. The train is made from two B set compartment coaches headed by a '4555' Class 2–6–2 tank.

CHAPTER 4
The archetypal station

In its heyday, the local station formed the main link with the outside world in a way difficult to visualize today. Not only did almost everyone arrive by train, but everything needed for life that could not be produced within a few miles of the town was also brought in by rail. As a direct result, the station was provided with numerous facilities to assist in the handling of the traffic. Whilst there could never be an absolutely typical station, the double track passing station serving a small to medium-sized town of between 3,000 and 8,000 inhabitants was extremely common and could be regarded as representative of the steam age.

In most cases the railway, when built, just skimmed the outskirts of the town to save the cost of purchasing the houses in its way. It could be anything up to three miles from the market square, while a greater distance would lead to the station name changing from ANYTOWN to ANYTOWN ROAD. In general, the station was built at the point where the railway crossed an existing main road on the assumption that most people would be able to find it with very little trouble. The main station buildings were situated on the town side and an approach road would be built to connect with the main road.

These buildings were generally of a substantial nature. It is fanciful to talk of a company's standard architecture, for what happened was that the major stations would normally be completely individual designs, occasionally intended to blend with the surrounding buildings and invariably designed to impress prospective passengers. The smaller stations would be built to a uniform pattern *for the section of line currently under construction*. On another line for the same company, the design could be radically different and, in certain larger projects, the design might vary according to the time of construction. Then, when stations were added, or extensively rebuilt, the latest fashion would be followed. Small independent concerns usually employed local architects on a one-off basis, but larger companies either retained a firm of architects as consultants, or had their own architectural division. Often the Chief Engineer would take it upon himself to design the buildings. The results, if you had a man of the calibre of Brunel in charge, could be superb, although they were frequently merely pedestrian.

The main station buildings held the station offices. These contained the entrance for passengers, which generally contained the ticket window. Often the entrance doubled as the general waiting room. Alongside was the booking office, where the station clerk worked. In small stations, this backed onto the parcels office, where the larger packages were received for transit and stored on arrival. Passengers could also leave luggage here. Double doors led both to the platform and the road to assist movement.

There might be a separate ladies' waiting room, from which the ladies' toilet led. Failing this, there would be a separate ladies' loo. The gents was not infrequently a lean-to structure at one end, used by passengers and staff. There was generally a porter's room and, if the station was fairly busy, a private office for the stationmaster; in smaller stations he used a corner of the booking office or his own living room.

Frequently the buildings incorporated the station house, though this could be a separate detached building adjacent to the approach road. This was the official residence of the stationmaster who was, in Victorian days, not merely expected to live on the job, but was also in practice on permanent call. The pay and perquisites were worth the inconvenience.

Awnings generally sprouted from the station building and might go some way along the platform. The footbridge was normally beyond the awnings in a small station, and might be open to the elements. Footbridges were generally of a standard pattern for the larger companies, while smaller lines tended to order from specialist manufacturers.

One generally found a shelter of some sort on the further platform. It might be an open wooden shelter, or it could be an elaborate brick or stone structure complete with awnings. The platforms were invariably connected by a barrow crossing to allow parcels and luggage to be transferred across the lines, and there would be at least one barrow or trolley somewhere on the platform.

From the turn of the century up to the late 1940s, a variety of slot machines were to be seen along the platform, offering chocolate bars for one old penny, giving your weight and even dispensing packets of cigarettes. These vanished once it was realized that no longer could one get such delights for a single, small coin. The platform ticket machine, located in the foyer, was a rare addition to this type of station. The platforms were liberally supplied with poster boards and, from the 1890s to the 1950s, would be well provided with enamelled iron advertisements for Oxo, Bovril, Mazawattee Tea, Stephen's Inks and other popular products. Commercial railway posters and enamelled signs are available in 7, 4 and 2mm scales and there is no excuse for not having these

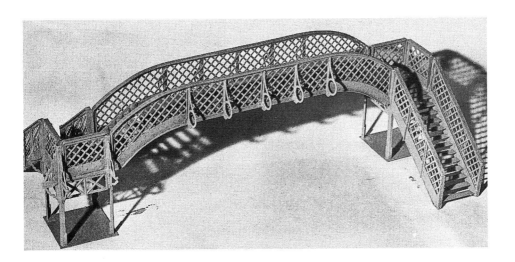

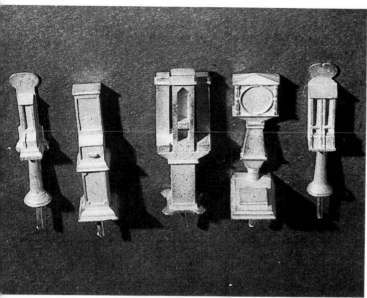

Left *Platform furniture, white metal castings for a variety of pre-war penny-in-the-slot machines that might be found on a steam age platform. Second from the left is the platform ticket machine which was, naturally, on the other side of the barrier.*

Below left *A small 4mm scale platform-mounted signal box made from a Ratio plastic kit.*

colourful features around the layout.

The next building in order of importance is the signal box. Throughout the steam age, from around 1860 onwards, the majority of lines were controlled by mechanically operated boxes communicating by a specialized form of telegraph. There was a practical limit to the distance over which mechanical control could function, so larger stations possessed two or more boxes, and possibly the odd ground frame as well.

The signal box was a standardized structure, designed in the company's signal works or by a specialist contractor on a modular basis, the length being determined by the number of levers that would be needed in the foreseeable future. Whilst most designs followed a common pattern, details differed. In particular the arrangement of roofing and the number and size of window panes were highly characteristic of company practice.

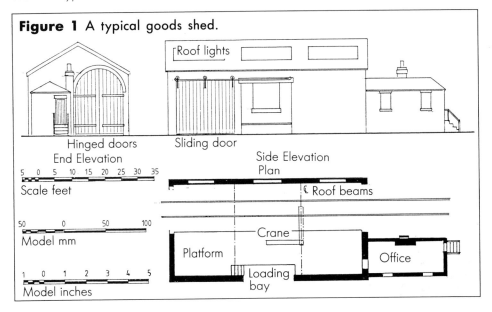

Figure 1 A typical goods shed.

Roof lights

Hinged doors · Sliding door
End Elevation · Side Elevation
Plan

Scale feet 5 0 5 10 15 20 25 30 35

Roof beams

Model mm 50 0 50 100

Crane

Platform

Office

Model inches 1 0 1 2 3 4 5

Loading bay

At most stations there was a goods shed. This was frequently a fairly large structure spanning one or more tracks, and Figure 1 shows the commonest design. The important factor is an internal platform to allow merchandise to be barrowed conveniently out of the wagons onto the loading ramp, and from there over the tailboard of a cart or lorry. There was, in many cases, an internal manually operated crane of medium capacity to assist in unloading heavy crates. A small office was provided to enable the paperwork to be done with some convenience; this was generally adjacent to the main building but might be accommodated inside the main structure, a more common arrangement in the larger sheds. The drawing shows a very small version, but on the majority of layouts this is about as large as one can find room for.

The goods shed was provided with strong doors so that the contents could be stored securely overnight. Even where the goods were delivered by the railway company, there was inevitably a hiatus between arrival and loading. When the goods were to be collected, there would be a delay whilst the consignee was notified. Remember, for much of the steam age there was no convenient telephone to contact a client.

Whilst there was a parcels office within the main building and a goods shed, on occasions these proved inadequate; furthermore, if the station handled a large amount of high-value merchandise by passenger train, neither of these locations was particularly secure against an opportunist thief. A separate lock-up store was the simple solution. Again, Figure 2 shows a brick structure, but since this would have been an addition to the station's facilities rather than a part of the original structures, it could well be in a different style.

Another small structure often found

alongside the platform is the lamp hut, also shown in Figure 2. This is an important feature for steam age stations, since even when the station itself was lit by gas and, later, electricity, the signals were almost always lit by oil lamps. Initially these needed refilling and trimming each day, but long-burning patterns were later developed which could be left burning for several days. Few readers will be aware of the messy nature of this task. For a start, it was almost impossible to prevent the outside of the oil reservoir from becoming coated with a thin film of oil, which collected all the muck and fluff in the atmosphere. This is bad enough inside the home, but a steam age signal was regularly engulfed in the exhaust from locomotives, which was predominantly steam but naturally contained a good deal of small particles of unburnt fuel, some of which ended up inside the lamp. Then the burning wick added its quota of mess. All this had to be cleaned away, then the reservoir needed to be replenished. As a result, the working area soon got filthy, whilst, in addition, the fumes were extremely pungent and, into the bargain, slightly toxic.

It didn't take very long for everyone to realize that this was a job best carried out away from the rest of the station offices. There were two approaches: a lamp room might be incorporated in the main buildings but isolated from the main structure with the door opening directly onto the platform, or the job could be done in a separate building. This approach had an added bonus in that the structure could incorporate a store for the kerosene drums, which, as a fire hazard, were best kept away from the main offices. I have shown, in Figure 2, a possible arrangement of such a building, located along the platform. The sketch suggests brick construction, but alternative materials were corrugated iron and asbestos sheeting. Timber lamp huts were very rare, since the fire risk was extremely high.

Another structure worthy of mention is the weighbridge. It is used, to this day, to determine the weight, and hence the value, of a lorry load, the principle being that the vehicle is weighed empty and the value noted on a docket, then, after loading, it is re-weighed, the new value being entered on the same docket, the difference representing the load. For

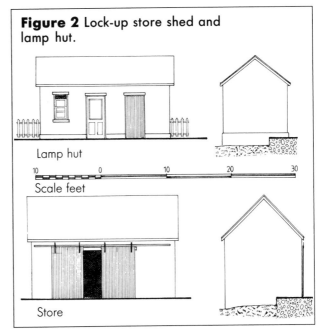

Figure 2 Lock-up store shed and lamp hut.

Lamp hut

10   0   10   20   30

Scale feet

Store

Below left *A substantial goods shed on Alan Smith's 3mm scale 'Hatfield Moor' layout.*

most of the steam age, the only weighbridge in a town was that at the railway station.

Figure 3 shows the general arrangement of a typical weighbridge. There is a large cast-iron platform in front of a small building which houses the steelyard. The steam age weighbridge was supported on a series of levers, so that the load could be measured against a very much smaller weight which slid along a beam. Generally, this was kept inside a building, though on occasions one could find the steelyard completely exposed on the side of a building with, at best, a short awning overhead. The old-fashioned lever system was very delicate, and if a load were run on the side instead of the end, there was a very distinct probability that the entire platform would come off the knife edges. This not only called for skilled attention,

but generally meant a visit from the local Weights and Measures Inspector to verify the accuracy of the machine; consequently, a low barrier, generally made up from worn bullhead rail, was provided to stop carters throwing the machine out of kilter.

It is not impossible to make a 4mm scale working model of the old-pattern weighbridge with lever bottomworks; indeed, Mike Sharman produced a white metal kit which could be persuaded to operate after a fashion. A good deal of careful craftsmanship would be needed and, in the final analysis, one would end up with a device that cannot be seen to operate. Of course, in the larger scales the situation is different, and it would be an interesting addition to a well-detailed O gauge shunting yard.

Many steam age stations possessed a small row of stables to house the horses

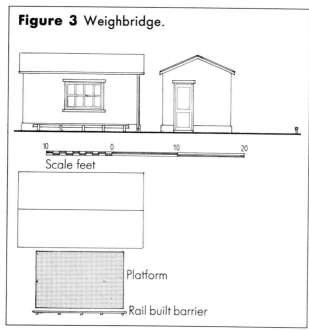

Figure 3 Weighbridge.

Scale feet

10   0   10   20

Platform

Rail built barrier

Right *Old coach bodies were often taken from their underframes and parked in the station yard for staff accommodation and other purposes. This Ratio kit, suitably doctored, shows one of these at the end of its life, battered, boarded and bereft.*

Below *The inevitable coal office and coal bins, made from a Wills 4mm scale plastic kit.*

used not only to deliver goods by company carts, but also to move wagons around the yard. There was often a number of miscellaneous huts for railway purposes spotted around the area, the most important of which were the platelayers' huts. These began life as timber shanties built to hold the tools secure and provide a place where the gangs could shelter or eat their meals. Later, brick-built huts came about, while the Southern Railway developed a neat

COAL OFFICE

pre-cast concrete unit that was designed to sit on a flat wagon for transit to the site, where it would be offloaded by a rail-mounted crane. This pattern spread elsewhere after nationalization, and as a precursor to the 'Portakabin' its utility is obvious.

The station would have a goods yard complete with a coal siding, and in most cases a cattle dock to handle not merely the transit of beasts from the farm, but also their arrival at a town for slaughter. I shall be going into more detail when I turn to the traffic of the steam age in later chapters. There could be a bay platform for terminating traffic, generally in conjunction with a nearby feeder branch.

There would frequently be a row of railway cottages for the staff, and where the station was well away from the town this was almost essential. They were substantial brick-built terraced houses

giving, even today, quite a reasonable level of accommodation, and when built they were definitely superior to the general run of artisans' dwellings.

I have, in Plan 1, shown a fairly typical double track through station in 4mm scale, arranged to fit into a garage. The curves are as large as possible to improve appearance and to offer the choice of EM or P4 as well as 00 gauge. It incorporates most of the features mentioned in this chapter and adds a factory with rail connection. The plan, though nowhere near to scale (it is about half the length of a normal through station) shows the sheer size of a thoroughgoing model of a steam age station. The platforms can only handle a four-coach train with comfort, but as local stopping trains on the main line rarely exceeded this length, all is well. The loops do slightly restrict the maximum train length and, given a little

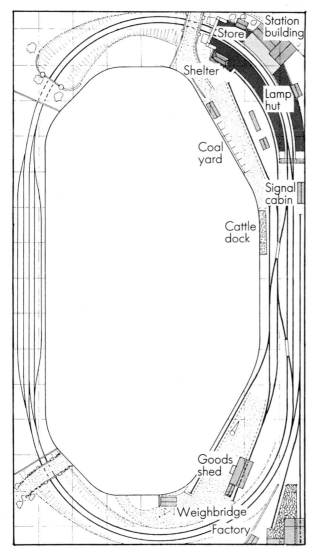

Plan 1 Double track through station for a space 15 ft × 8 ft 6 in in 4mm scale.

more room, could with advantage be lengthened and increased in number.

Operationally, this is a 'watching the trains go by' model, but a little variety is brought about not only by the bay road, with its corresponding reversing central road in the loops, but also by the arrangement of the goods yard which calls for a good deal of shunting. To assist this, I have shown a run-round loop in the main yard; this allows the train engine to get on either end of a wagon, whilst an additional trailing crossover on the main line also provides run-round facilities.

CHAPTER 5
Following the prototype

On the face of it, nothing could be more realistic than modelling an actual prototype station. After all, we wouldn't dream of building a 'Castle' Class locomotive on a 4-4-2 chassis and giving it a parallel boiler, would we? Well, on reflection, we might: Meccano Ltd did! However, it is a good deal easier to discover sufficient information to build a model of a locomotive than it is to do the same for a steam age station.

Forty years ago things were different; the stations were there, and it was just a matter of packing camera, notebook and pencil, plus a few sandwiches and a thermos flask of coffee, and buying a ticket to the chosen prototype. Even so, details were altered over the years and the fact that there was an awning over the entrance in 1948 didn't necessarily mean it was there in 1900, or for that matter in 1952! Fortunately, a good deal of information was recorded and published, first as articles in long-out-of-print

Mike Cook's 'Dawlish' was an early essay in prototype modelling. The original station lent itself to accurate reproduction but operationally it was devoid of interest; the goods yard was small, cramped and offered no opportunity for serious shunting.

Maurice Deane's 1950 model of Hemyock station, a very close copy of the original. The line had two points of note: the curvature was excessively sharp, and there was a milk depot at the terminus. This is the only example I know of such a structure on a branch; normally they were located on main lines, since the milk was brought to the factory by road.

magazines, then as rather more accessible books. As I've mentioned earlier, a lot more has gone missing with the passage of time.

Nevertheless there is enough information readily to hand to enable one to make an 80 per cent accurate replica of any of several hundred British stations,

providing one has the room available. A little digging about will produce quite a lot more information, but we come to the key question — is it worthwhile? Rather than talk in generalities, I shall consider a specific station, Lyme Regis, partly because I happen to know the locality well, but mainly because it is a

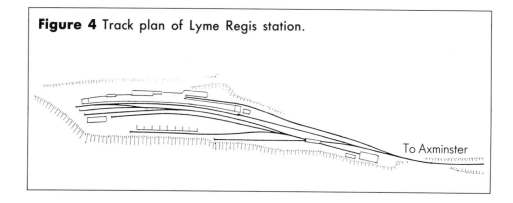

Figure 4 Track plan of Lyme Regis station.

To Axminster

good example of the snags inherent in this particular theme.

We begin with one distinct advantage: a good deal has been written about the branch, with the result that one can quickly get hold of a good deal of information. The layout plan (Figure 4) shows a simple, straightforward station which, on the face of it, should be easy to reproduce in model form. However, what you can't do is reproduce it faithfully in a restricted area for, despite the fact that it was commendably compact, it was able to hold six coaches.

A fairly intensive search through my library failed to produce any drawings of the station buildings or any clear details of the engine shed, so one might have a few problems. This is only the start. Lyme Regis was for much of its life the haunt of the surviving Adams Radial 4-4-2 tanks, lovely locomotives by any standards, but even though each of the three differed in detail from its sisters, one is still left with a rather restricted locomotive stud. The trouble is that everyone knows this! Other locomotives did run over the branch, including a GWR '14xx' for a couple of weeks, a BR Standard Class '2' 2-6-2T at the end, and an odd selection of LSWR and LB&SCR small tanks in the early days. The trouble is that at any given period, there was just one type on offer. Things look a little less promising, but let's press on.

The branch began life as the independent Axminster and Lyme Regis Light Railway, which had its effect on the arrangements at Axminster (Figure 5). The branch platform was on the up side of the line, which not only meant that the line had to cross over the LSWR tracks but also that the trains terminated on the far side from the station building. The interesting point is that this was 'Railway No 2' of the light railway; 'Railway No 1' came in on the other side. The connection was only used for goods transfer and fell into disuse, being removed in 1915. The prototype plan shows Axminster as it was when the branch was built, with both lines in existence. It will be seen that there was no direct connection between the branch platform and the main line, transfer from the branch being made through a long siding. Getting the through coaches from the down main to the branch involved a good deal of shunting, although fortunately, in the reverse direction, things were a little easier.

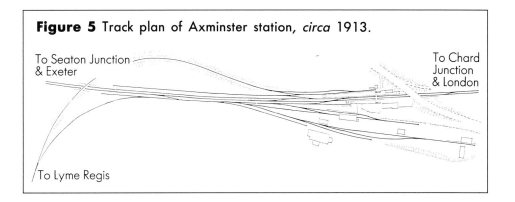

Figure 5 Track plan of Axminster station, *circa* 1913.

To Seaton Junction & Exeter

To Chard Junction & London

To Lyme Regis

The facade of the Midland/ Somerset & Dorset station at Bath, a very impressive building backing on to an equally impressive train shed which boasted two platforms and a rather sparse service. This is an excellent example of the way an infiltrating company would attempt to convince passengers that the new line meant business.

In complete contrast to Bath we have the entire buildings of Heathfield, a timber station building with an abbreviated awning and small extensions, together with a lock-up goods shed, also in timber.

Prototype for everything; this pair of back-to-back buffer stops were at Chippenham for many years, providing two end-on bay platforms for local services. Today, HSTs thunder along this bit of track, restored to main-line duties.

As the through train would be headed by two Radials, the procedure was to stop the train on the overbridge and detach the first locomotive. This would run down into the bay and back into the transfer road. Once this was done, the remaining loco would ease the train gently down the gradient and, at long last, both passengers for Axminster could get out. The first loco would now back onto the train and, once couplings and brake hoses had been dealt with, would pull the train into the transfer siding. With any luck, the up train would soon arrive and the coaches would be backed onto it in a couple of minutes.

If you set out to model Lyme Regis in 4mm scale, you'll need at least the full length of a normal garage to do so, and even then train lengths will be curtailed. Having done so, you'll end up with a very restricted operating pattern and an even more restricted locomotive stud. However, if you included Axminster the resulting model would be much more attractive. Unfortunately, whereas Lyme will fit into a garage with a little squeeze, Axminster won't. It's not merely that you'll not be able to get the full length of train into the platforms — one can live with this — it's also that the prototype station approach is quite long and the yard sprawls in the usual generous fashion of the steam age station built on the edge of the town where land was cheap. The station, incidentally, is still on the edge of the town, and the railway has formed a barrier to expansion in that direction. However, it is possible to keep the basic pattern of main line and branch pointwork intact and create a reasonable facsimile of the prototype which is, in my opinion, sufficiently different to not be Axminster at all. This is

not necessarily a disadvantage, since by using the prototype as the basis for a station, we have an authentic track arrangement but are no longer tied down to the exact limitations of the actual station.

Plan 2 (overleaf) is drawn to fit comfortably into a standard garage in 4mm scale. The minimum radius is 24 in, and there is room to work six-coach trains on the main line. The branch terminus, 'Kings Ash', is a fairly close copy of Lyme Regis so far as the track is concerned, though it is a good 15 per cent shorter and can only manage a four-coach train. The loco shed is based on that popular prototype at Tetbury, with the water tank over the shed end, while the station building and goods shed are basically those at the original.

'Flaxminster' follows the basic track layout of Axminster, but is greatly reduced in length. As it is an imaginary station, I've added a milk depot; on the prototype these existed at Seaton Junction and Chard Junction and provide an interesting addition to the traffic workings, but more to the point the depot allows us, in our limited space, to simulate what was a very important part of traffic working on the Western division of the Southern.

The goods yard is very much simplified, and the station approach is only a shadow of the original. The footbridge has been moved and there is no room for the down platform extension beneath the overbridge. The prototype, in steam days, was anything but convenient; the main business was carried out on the shorter up platform which, apart from a lean-to wooden hut, was devoid of shelter so that waiting for the London train on a wet morning was no joke. In addition, one had to manhandle any luggage over the footbridge. The model

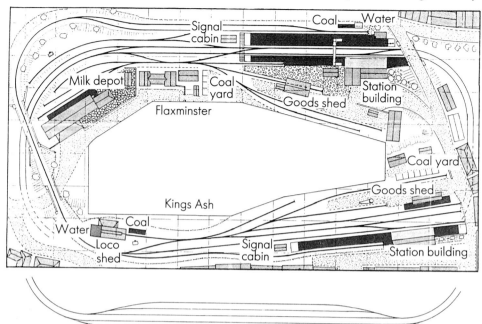

Signal
cabin

Coal   Water

Milk depot   Coal
yard

Station
building

Goods shed

Flaxminster

Coal yard

Goods shed

Kings Ash

Water   Coal

Loco
shed

Signal
cabin

Station building

Plan 2 'Flaxminster', a
layout based loosely on
the Axminster-Lyme
Regis combination for a
space 15 ft × 8 ft in
4mm scale.

*A corner of York station, a
pleasing array of glazed
awnings and other architectural follies close to the
main porte-cochère. This
could be an excellent starting point for a model.*

signal box is located where the second BR-built box was erected, not long before the line was singled and all signals and points disappeared.

I have shown a simple set of loops under the branch terminus. This could pose a few operating problems if one was to try to work through trains and attach milk tank wagons to the local trains, and if anyone is inspired to model something on these lines, it would be well worth while spending a good deal of time working out how best to develop the hidden sidings to allow the necessary interchange in the space that is actually available.

Almost the only scenic features that are even roughly aligned with the prototype are the two bridges which serve to delimit the visible area of the main line. In the case of the road bridge, the angle is smaller than on the prototype, but I have retained the suggestion that the down platform extends beyond. The main road remains at a high level and a fringe of houses, shops or what have

you helps to provide a scenic break. These are, needless to say, not on the prototype and, furthermore, we have that all too common arrangement on a model, where it is far quicker to walk between the two stations than to take the train!

Limitations of space restrict main-line trains to seven coaches. Don't worry that these won't fit into the up platform, as the prototype express didn't get into Axminster's up platform either! Down trains, of course, have their tails neatly tucked under the bridge. The basic operation of the prototype can be followed with reasonable fidelity and given a little more room to provide a more extensive set of hidden loops with room for remarshalling, one could come fairly close to the actual working timetable. What's more, you can enjoy the sight of the 'A.C.E.' or the 'Devon Belle' thundering through your railway room, which to my mind is the best way of recapturing the full glory of the steam age in miniature.

CHAPTER 6
Main-line modelling

In my opinion, the first choice for a steam age modeller should be a main-line layout. Not only will this enable you to run the lovely large express locomotives that are so readily available today in 00 and N, but you can also, with very little trouble, justify almost any type of traffic you fancy. Almost everything went onto the main line.

There is one serious snag. Unless you set your period before 1900, you have to face the fact that a main-line passenger train will not be less than eight bogie coaches in length, and could go as high as 15 vehicles, each 60 ft to 64 ft in length. Even this was not a record, and 22- to 24-coach trains were frequently run on the LNER during the 1939–1945 fracas, but as they didn't fit into King's Cross either, we can ignore them. As a matter of record, a 14-coach train plus a Bulleid 'Pacific' didn't quite fit into Waterloo, but even if we merely talk of eight to ten coaches we still need, in 4mm scale, platforms between 8 and 10 ft in length and, taking as a rough rule of thumb that a station is not less than 2.5 times its maximum train length, we are talking of 25 to 30 ft long stations, which is rather larger than the normal home can accommodate. One satisfactory

solution is to opt for N gauge, where the length required is roughly halved and, in the space afforded by a standard garage, allows eight- to ten-coach trains to be handled. This meets most needs, since the very long trains were confined to a limited number of routes.

This lack of space is not a new phenomenon. If anything, the problem was much more acute in the early days of the hobby when Gauges 1 and 2 were the mainstay and 0 gauge was provided for minimum space railways. Even though most enthusiasts of those times lived in what are today extremely large houses, the usual attic room that was employed for the hobby rarely exceeded 24 ft in its longest dimension. Of course one read then, as one does today, of cases where individuals were able to afford a really large railway room, but these are the exceptions.

There are many people who maintain that a 4mm scale main-line layout must be a group project. This can help ease many difficulties, although it creates others, but even with the resources of a long-established club to fall back on, it is still difficult to construct a layout on which full-length main-line trains can be operated realistically. Most such layouts

Above *Bradcaster station building on Norman Eagles' O gauge layout was based closely on a design by Henry Greenly. Although compact enough to fit into a tiny space, the model successfully apes the style of a much larger structure.*

Below *One way of fitting a large and impressive station building into the limited space of the normal railway room is to build it in low relief across the tracks, on an overbridge. This impressive block was at Geoff Bigmore's 'Bigston', and created the illusion that the terminus was, in reality, a through station.*

on the exhibition circuit are limited to eight-coach rakes. However, to suggest that the lone wolf working in 4mm scale must eschew the delights of a main-line system, forget any hope of running trains that do not look out of place behind a large express locomotive and stick tamely to the more limited locomotive potential of the branch is, I consider, not merely a negative view, but is damaging to the hobby's development. Our predecessors managed well

enough and were content with trains of three or four coaches to represent a major express.

I therefore offer two approaches out of the many suited to a standard suburban garage, a space that is reasonably easy to acquire for the hobby. The first, Plan 3, is for a middling-sized terminus capable of handling, in comfort, a six-coach train. As can be seen, there is a good deal of room beyond the buffers so it would not be all that difficult to allow

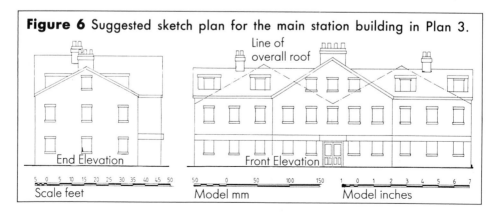

Figure 6 Suggested sketch plan for the main station building in Plan 3.

End Elevation

Line of overall roof

Front Elevation

Scale feet

Model mm

Model inches

Left *A section of the Midland main line, reproduced in 2mm scale by members of the Model Railway Club on their superb 'Chiltern Green' layout. A faithful replica of the prototype, this was the centrepiece of a superb example of a railway in deep landscape.*

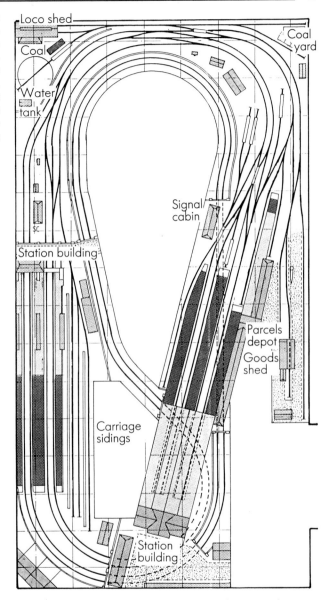

Loco shed

Coal

Water tank

Coal yard

Signal cabin

Station building

SC

Parcels depot

Goods shed

Carriage sidings

Station building

Plan 3 Large main-line scheme in 4mm scale based around extensive terminal facilities for a space 15 ft × 8 ft.

for an extra coach, if so desired. However, the plan is drawn to fit a 15 ft × 8 ft area, which is slightly smaller than most garages — my own is nearly 18 ft in length. Since every 11 in of additional

length can mean another coach, it is clear that the same plan, in a slightly larger garage, could easily handle an eight-coach train.

Or, to be more accurate, more than six

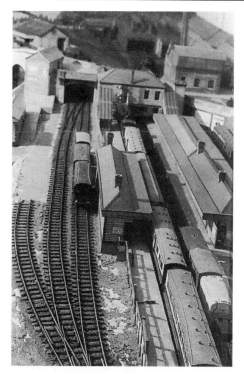

such trains, which puts the matter into a slightly different perspective. As drawn, the layout requires at least 36 coaches to reach its potential, and the full capacity is over 50. This is not only a fairly hefty collection by any standards, but is only the start. There is also need for up to a dozen bogie parcels vans and around 40 to 60 goods wagons before we add the minimum dozen locomotives needed to work the trains. This, incidentally, is

Left *The main station on Jack Nelson's HO gauge LNWR layout, built in the early '50s. The station buildings are typical of an LNWR through station built to handle growing traffic along the busy West Coast route.*

Below *In the steam age, lineside industries were almost always rail connected. Here we see a small timber yard with its own siding. Logs are being unloaded from a pair of bolster wagons.*

why I have not shown any hidden loops for additional train storage; I came to the conclusion that the capacity of the line was probably big enough as it was and would stretch the resources of most enthusiasts.

The layout follows the justly popular 'out and back' format, the majority of the main line forming a very large reversing loop. This type of layout not only provides for ease of operation, but also affords a reasonable length of unencumbered main line over which one's trains can romp away. Agreed, in looping back on itself in this fashion one does, in plan, loose all sense of realism but if, as I suggest, an urban setting is employed, the overall effect is quite good, since even today, when so many lines have gone, one finds plenty of places in our larger cities where several lines run close together. In the steam age this was extremely common and a maze of tracks at several levels, linked by brick retaining walls, certainly provides a superb setting for steam age trains.

As this is essentially a single-handed layout, all operating interest is concentrated on the terminus. There are four main platforms, one shorter bay outside the overall roof and an adjacent parcels depot. The goods yard is behind the station, set at a slight angle, a common arrangement with city termini.

Goods facilities are very cut down, I'm afraid, but here we come up against one of the inevitable compromises required to create a practical layout. For a start, the yard is at extreme reach and auto-coupling is absolutely essential, so even were more space available, it would still be undesirable to extend the number of roads since this could render the yard all but inaccessible. This is a bad idea, for derailments are commonplace in goods yards, on the prototype as well as the model. I'm all for aping full-sized practice wherever possible, but there are times when this can go a little too far. Although it looks as if there is a double track entry to the yard, in practice the two roads serve as independent shunting tracks combined with run-round loops. A small coal depot is tucked into the far corner, but if you preferred to turn one of the three goods shed roads into a coal road, this corner piece could serve a factory.

The parcels depot is a little easier to shunt, and is arranged to permit vans to be run into the shortest platform in the station itself; this would, I suggest, be reserved for this type of traffic, while the three longer platforms and the bay would take care of the main passenger service.

Locomotive facilities are a trifle sparse, being a two-road shed and a turntable. Most of the locomotive standing is provided by spurs at the platform ends, and I envisage the shed being used to stable a couple of spare engines, the depot's main function being to turn tender locomotives.

A simple four-platform through station is provided, partly as scenic effect and partly to allow the trains to come to a halt for polarity reversal for the loop. I've shown an over-track station building typical of outer suburban designs, with rudimentary waiting facilities on the platforms. The carriage sidings are alongside with a crossover link to release the shunting loco.

A terminus provides ample operating potential and is therefore justly popular, but, as an alternative, the junction station with its attendant feeder branch also offers an excellent way of reproducing the delights of the steam age main line.

I've already in the previous chapter shown one example of this particular theme, and in Plan 4 I show another approach which relies on the fact that all commercial ready-to-run 00 gauge stock will go round an 18 in radius curve with ease, although it looks rather odd whilst doing so. Indeed, the 24 in curve I normally use when drawing plans for 4mm scale is still rather too tight for good visual effect. There is a very simple answer, however — hide the sharp corners and ensure that all tracks in the open have gentle curves.

Once again, the plan is intended to fit into a garage, but this time I have made it possible to include the car, providing, that is, you are content to keep to a 'super-mini' and set the baseboards high enough not only to allow the bonnet to go underneath, but for the door to open as fully as possible under the framing. It is going to be something of a tight squeeze!

There are several interesting scenic features. Townscapes are provided at each end of the junction station to hide the curves, and I've suggested dummy

tracks to create the illusion that the main line is virtually straight. Another small town scene covers the curve under the branch terminus and provides room for a station forecourt.

At the far end we have a gently curving main line backed by the wide sweep of the branch, whilst across the entrance there is a large masonry bridge spanning a river. I've included a sketch for a possible design, which follows Brunel at a respectful distance. The baseboards at this end of the layout would have to be dismantled to get the car in; it would, I think, be a good idea to take down the throat of the junction as well to give you room to get out of the car. A 9 ft wide garage would be much better.

A battery of storage loops is provided under the branch terminus; two roads are arranged to provide reversal, but as there are no easy facilities for turning tender locomotives, this facility is of necessity limited, as for that matter is the clearance between the branch terminus and the hidden tracks, which will preclude any extensive re-arrangement of trains. There is, however, storage capacity for three main-line trains in each direction, express passenger, local passenger and freight, which is sufficient to provide a pleasing sequence of trains on the model.

These hidden storage sidings, the fiddle yard, are the key to simulating prototype operation within the limited space of a practical model railway. They represent the rest of the prototype railway system and, depending on your own preferences and the operating pattern you select, can either be simple storage loops where made-up trains lurk, waiting their brief moment of glory

Left *The layout at Par was a useful one for model purposes, being a three-platform station with the further road also used as a goods reception as well as providing a line for terminating services.*

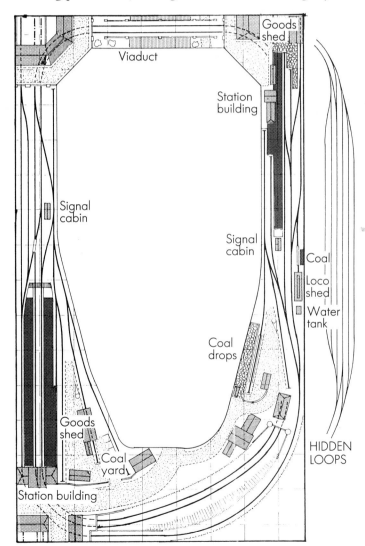

Plan 4 Junction station with branch line scheme for a space 15 ft × 8 ft in 4mm scale.

during the run around the visible tracks, or a place where stock is re-arranged offstage to present, to the viewer, a more interesting array of trains. I have used theatrical terminology of intent, for we are in the business of creating an illusion, in far less space than a prototype station would occupy, of the entire might and glory of the steam age railway. Shakespeare's prologue to *Henry V* is remarkably apposite to our hobby.

NER 'Atlantic' passing over the level crossing on a superb 4mm scale model of Wylam set in the early years of the century.

Figure 7 River bridge, based loosely on Brunel designs, to cross the entrance section in Plan 4.

Scale feet

CHAPTER 7
The great iron roof

As the steam age got under way, the train shed became a major feature of all principal stations, and many quite minor ones. Spanning several tracks, it soared high above the platforms, protecting the passengers and staff from rain, hail and snow and, not infrequently, acting as an effective wind tunnel into the bargain. A few were wooden — the Brunel-inspired structures on the GWR are well known and popular with modellers — but the majority were iron. Although, initially, many were brightly painted, before long the accumulated soot and dirt inseparable from steam dulled their glory, the glass became begrimed and

Brunel's masterpiece in timber, the hammerbeam roof of the Old station at Temple Meads, Bristol. This photo was taken on a Sunday in the early '50s, when the station was deserted. After a period when it covered a car park, the structure is at last getting the treatment it deserves.

the light, airy character that impressed so many journalists in the early days of the railway was forgotten.

However, even dirt and grime could not hide the soaring glory of the great iron roofs. Many writers have resorted to purple prose, and those with a taste in this direction will doubtless have seen examples. For my part I prefer simply to admire those roofs that remain whilst applauding the care that has been lavished on some of the finer examples in these

not altogether iconoclastic times and admiring the occasional example of a modern train shed, such as the pleasing one at Leeds.

The important thing is that the train shed is part and parcel of the steam age, and should equally be part of any thoroughgoing steam age model. Although a good model of a train shed calls for a certain amount of work, it is rather less than is involved in the construction of accurate platform awnings.

It is also far less obstructive, since it is not unduly difficult to arrange for all or part of the roof to lift off to provide access to the tracks.

There are, moreover, a number of kits on the market, and although these do tend to make it imperative to design the station around the kit, manufacturers nowadays have set out the spans to cover a reasonable width of track and platform so little compromise is required.

Train shed roofs fall into two main categories, pitched and curved. The overwhelming majority of timber roofs are pitched, for fairly obvious reasons. The only major curved timber roof of the steam age was at King's Cross, where the timbers did their level best to push the station walls over, as a result of which the present iron roof was substituted. For amateur construction, the pitched roof is to be preferred, not merely because the roof principals are

fairly easy to model, using commercial angle section or built-up girders made from styrene sheet, but also, and more significantly, because the glazing is much more straightforward. Having said that, an elliptical arched roof such as the magnificent example at St Pancras is a challenge to the keen modelmaker, though for the majority one of the commercial plastic kits, most of which are for circular section roofs, is a sound choice.

One problem with train sheds is the uncoupling of locomotives at the far end. The provision of a reliable auto-coupling might seem an essential, but even where three-link couplers are preferred, there is a fairly simple solution. The coupling hook on the tender, or on both ends of a tank locomotive, is slightly modified, and the coupling itself is made solid. Figure 8 shows how it can be bent from a single length of wire. Two ears are soldered to lie alongside

__Top left__ The Brunel timber roof was more common on the main line than at branch termini, contrary to popular belief. The train shed at Frome lay over tracks which, at one time, formed the main route to the West Country.

__Above left__ This train shed roof for 4mm scale began life as several Pola kits for N gauge. A little extra height was obtained by fitting a clerestory to the roof. In the larger scale the plastic mouldings have the air of delicacy that characterized the prototype iron roof.

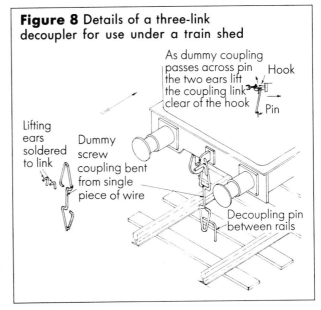

Figure 8 Details of a three-link decoupler for use under a train shed

As dummy coupling passes across pin the two ears lift the coupling link clear of the hook

Hook

Pin

Lifting ears soldered to link

Dummy screw coupling bent from single piece of wire

Decoupling pin between rails

Nottingham Castle was the principal station on Norman Eagles' 'Sherwood' layout and as such possessed a magnificent train shed. As the line was clockwork powered, access to the locomotives was of paramount importance, so the girders supported two large sheets of glass, painted to represent individual panes, which were lifted carefully off at the start of each running session.

the hook, and a trip mounted between the rails a loco length from the buffers. The coaches are hooked onto the locomotive and, when the train runs in, they are automatically detached.

It is also possible to arrange for one side of the roofing to lift off for operation. Once again, this is best done with a pitched roof, but even a curved roof is amenable to this sort of treatment, providing one uses a sheet of thin perspex, moulded to the correct contour, as the foundation of the roofing. As an alternative, the shed can be fairly short so that only the locomotive is covered, its purpose being mainly to cover the concourse and, of course, to impress the viewer.

The train shed is an excellent way of making what is really quite a small mainline terminus appear impressive, and brings us to ways of fitting steam-age main-line prototypes into small areas, which is, I feel, a side of the hobby that has been sadly neglected. It is my belief that a busy double track line is far better suited to a restricted space than

the more conventional branch prototype. Although on the face of it a single track branch, with its simple station plans, appears easier to compact, the open nature of the setting is very difficult to reproduce on a small baseboard. It's little use copying a rural prototype, for if you do you tend to need baseboards around 3 ft in width if the setting is to look right. An urban railway is hemmed in by buildings, it often runs on brick arches or between retaining walls and most of the space in between is full of trackwork. It also has another virtue — larger locomotives do not look out of place.

Plan 5 is for a terminus situated along one side of a garage, leaving ample room for the car. The odd shape is easily explained, for my own garage had just such a kink and the design is an exploration for a possible project of my own. The train shed is shown in some detail in Figure 9, which shows the general shape of the supporting walls for the shed. I have drawn an open arch; this is fairly unlikely, but exists to give a better view of the trains, a case of modeller's licence. You could substitute a glazed panel.

The station design is fairly conventional, apart from the incline to the loco depot. Several main-line termini had separate roads leading to the depot, allowing light engine movements to and from the shed to be clear of the main line, but my inspiration is an early model, Bill Banwell's 'Maybank'. The need to service steam locomotives at not more than ten-hour intervals made it essential to have such depots handy to main termini, as explained in a later chapter. This creates some difficulties, hence the high-level location which also serves to cover the curve in the corner. It is much smaller than one would like, but better than nothing at all.

I have not provided a run-round in the platforms for a very good reason — I don't want to cut down the storage facilities at the expense of additional pointwork. It is much simpler to have extra locomotives to take the train out

again. In pre-war days, run-round loops were provided for one good reason, that locomotives were so costly that few enthusiasts had anywhere near enough. Today we usually have too many! This also allows us to use the train shed for its original purpose, to act as a carriage shed.

The train length is set by the size of the train turntable, and this, as drawn, is less than the longer platform, but when one has a locomotive at each end of the train, as is implicit in this type of station, the extra space is taken up very nicely.

Getting trains in and out of the goods yard involves a good deal of shunting and requires one of the platform roads to be clear for part of the time. As a result, the timetable requires careful planning so that freight trains arrive when the platform is clear. This makes the working much more interesting and puts a penalty on merely playing trains, for one is apt to get things in such a tangle that the need to schedule train movements becomes obvious. This is strictly in ac-

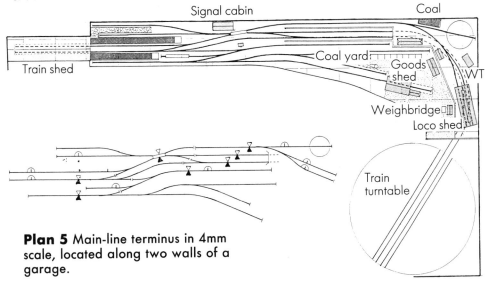

Plan 5 Main-line terminus in 4mm scale, located along two walls of a garage.

Figure 9 Details of the train shed for Plan 5.

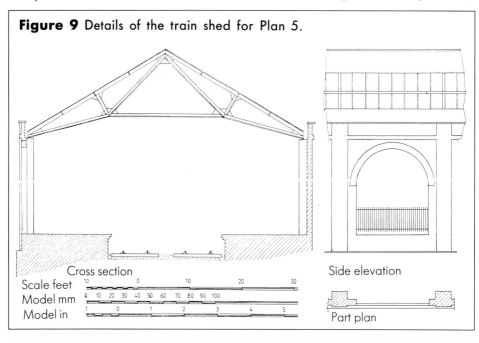

Cross section

Scale feet

Model mm

Model in

Side elevation

Part plan

Figure 10 Main station building for Plan 6.

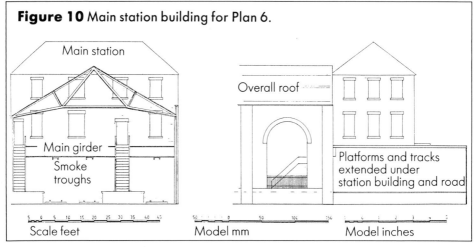

Main station

Main girder

Smoke troughs

Overall roof

Platforms and tracks
extended under
station building and road

Scale feet

Model mm

Model inches

cordance with prototype practice.

Plan 6 is intended to fit into a medium-sized bedroom, leaving space for a bed and a couple of other items of furniture. Indeed, the room is one I had as a young

man and if I'd known then what I know now, I'd probably have built something along these lines.

The terminus has three platform roads, arranged on a 3 ft radius curve.

The third platform road also serves as the goods arrival, departure and head-shunt. It isn't ideal, but I wanted to keep the width down. We are limited on this layout to trains of no more than 3 ft 9 in in length, which appears to restrict us to three-coach trains. There is one simple way round this particular difficulty, and that is to go back in period to around the turn of the century when coaches and locomotives were shorter.

I include a block diagram of the main station buildings. Although the model station is a terminus, the scenic development suggests a through station, with the tracks running under the main road. This provides space for the station building in a very restricted site and also explains why there is no release crossover, which would be present on the prototype. In a restricted model it is better to eliminate this feature and use either a station pilot or another train engine to take the stock out again. In this way, both roads can be occupied without making operation difficult.

This arrangement would seem to call for a reliable uncoupler, but even this will need some careful spotting if the rear bufferbeam of the train loco is to be aligned on the ramp. As usual, there is a simple solution — the station building and road are built on a piece of 4mm ply and lift out. The locomotives are now completely accessible and it is im-material whether you use auto-couplers or the three-link variety. There is also an added advantage. As the road unit is not fixed, you can knock up a simple struc-ture at the outset, then, at your leisure, make an elaborate-looking building away from the layout. The arrangement

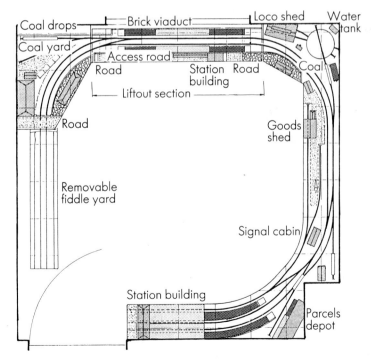

Plan 6 Double track main-line layout for a space 9 ft × 8 ft 6 in in 4mm scale.

of the model means that the main station building's façade is very prominent, and so a really impressive model is called for.

Figure 11 shows one approach to the parcels depot design. This is supposed to be a between-the-wars ferro-concrete-framed building with brick infill. Two roller shutter doors lead out onto the loading platform which is provided with a cantilevered canopy. The design is faintly reminiscent of the warehouses erected in the late '30s in Victoria Dock. I've opted for a modern design since, on this awkward site, a flat-roofed building is a much easier proposition, but it does mean that the model is set in the inter-war period.

The goods yard is conventional, comprising two roads for general merchandise with an over-track shed. In the cor-

ner we have a 60 ft diameter turntable feeding a truncated shed. A further loco spur is provided. I know it is reached by a facing point and is technically wrong, but in a tight site like this you have to provide what loco standing you can in the space you have available.

There is a removable section over the window, which not only gives access for cleaning, but also allows a little more room in the bedroom when the layout is not in use. As is my wont, I have put a viaduct over this section. However, it is a very special viaduct, a series of brick arches carrying the second station. I've provided a sketch plan of part of this section (Figure 12) to give you a rough idea of what I have in mind. The model is based loosely on the stations found around South London, and the block

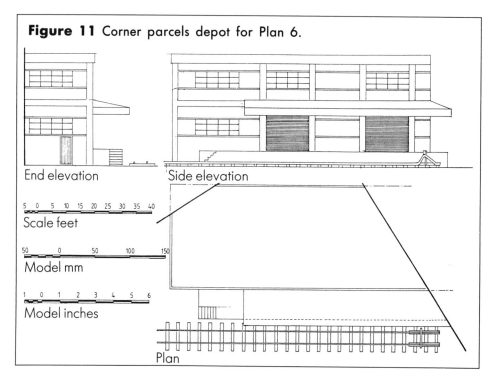

Figure 11 Corner parcels depot for Plan 6.

End elevation

Side elevation

Scale feet
5 0 5 10 15 20 25 30 35 40

Model mm
50 0 50 100 150

Model inches
1 0 1 2 3 4 5 6

Plan

Figure 12 Viaduct and intermediate station details for Plan 6.

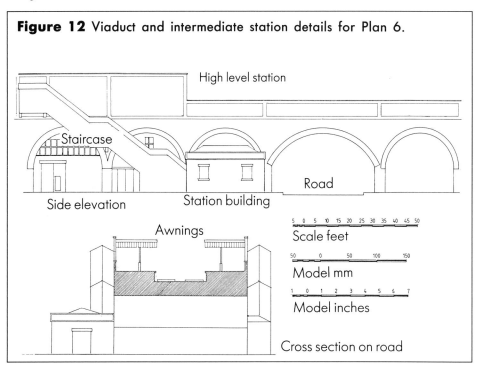

High level station

Staircase

Side elevation

Station building

Road

Awnings

Scale feet
5 0 5 10 15 20 25 30 35 40 45 50

Model mm
50 0 50 100 150

Model inches
1 0 1 2 3 4 5 6 7

Cross section on road

plan is more concerned with the overall arrangement than the precise details. The only factor to bear in mind is that the arches of this type of viaduct are normally set at 35 ft centres. The plan shows an access road along the front of the occupied arches. The rear will not normally be seen, so you could omit all details, but with the section being removable the possibility of exhibiting must be kept in mind.

The final corner is devoted to the coal yard, with both coal drops and surface coal bins. A trailing crossover allows for slightly more elaborate shunting at this point. I've sketched in a few industrial buildings around the line and, needless to say, the backdrop should either be low-relief factories or house backs.

Both schemes are limited to a relative-ly small number of trains, though as the operation can easily become quite intensive, there is little likelihood that they will soon lose interest. There might be more problems if one is either a prolific builder of locomotives and coaches, or is an inveterate hoarder of models and would like to have more on show.

It is not always realized that, if we exclude the locomotives and rolling-stock, only a few relatively small items on a model need be conspicuously dated, or aligned to a specific company's practice. When your space is limited, it pays to wring every drop you can from the little room you have, and if, by judicious exchange of small details, you can have a different company or period, so much the better!

CHAPTER 8
Following the branch lines

Strictly speaking, a branch line is a less important route branching off the main trunk line. It can have double track and take the heaviest classes of locomotive and support an intensive service. An excellent example is the branch off the old GWR main line at Newton Abbot (strictly speaking, Aller Junction) to Torquay and Paignton, a very busy double track line. However, modellers have long worked on the formula: Branch = single track + tank locomotives.

This is probably a more useful practical distinction and one I see no reason to fault. So, when I speak of branch lines, I refer to secondary routes, normally single track and almost invariably rural in nature.

It is sometimes said that the branch line station is more readily built to scale in a small area. Not so, for many branch termini occupied rather more space than quite a few city stations for the simple reason that land was still relatively cheap when they were built and promoters left room for later expansion. The real advantage of the branch line as the basis for a model lies in the fact that passenger trains were from one to four coaches in length and station layouts were fairly simple. As a result, it is possible to reduce the length of most branch line stations by as much as 50 per cent without having to omit a single siding or alter the point formations one iota. Into the bargain, you can run accurate replicas of the normal passenger trains to the authentic working timetable.

On the debit side, you can't, on a compressed branch line model, run the correct size goods train, leastways not if you are modelling one before 1950 when goods trains could run to over 20 wagons. Even more to the point, you will find it rather difficult to account for the presence of a large tender locomotive unless you choose to model one of the major single track branches which led to popular resorts.

The classic branch line model is the terminus–fiddle yard scheme fitted into the corner of a room, an example of which I have shown in Plan 7. Inevitably the model is highly compressed, and if modelled to scale (if one can speak of scale when dealing with an imagined prototype), it would need over three times the length shown.

The plan is shown broken down into individual baseboard sections but I am assuming that, for most of the time, it would be permanently erected in a cor-

Above *Most branch layouts have little unencumbered main line, but Ken Payne, on his second EM gauge GWR layout, found room for a good stretch and here we see the all too typical GWR '14XX' plus trailer combination so popular as a secondary branch train.*

Right *Frank Colson's 4mm scale branch reflects its period, the late 1940s, with the now obsolete outside third current collection. This early compact lay-out fitted into a large cupboard, yet could be operated intensively in a prototypical fashion.*

Above *During the 1970s, Alan Wright's 'Cheviotdale' was a popular visitor to Northern exhibitions. Very compact, it was a simple continuous single track NER branch model with an extensive set of sliding storage roads which allowed a very intensive service of varied trains to be run. Part of these sidings can be seen behind the elaborate tunnel mouth, one of the Faller 'Lorelei' pair, as much at home in northern England as the prototype is alongside the Rhine.*

Below *A branch goods pulls into the loop at Cheviotdale.*

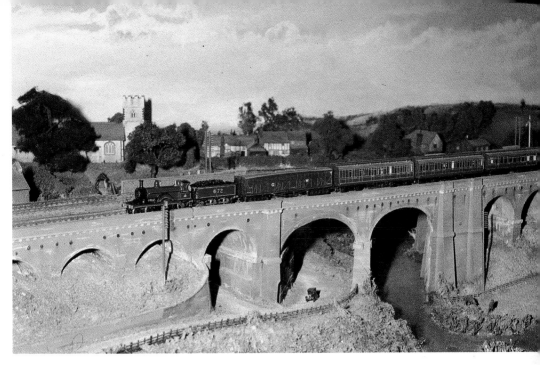

The steam age in miniature

Above *Steam-age grandeur. A fine 2mm scale model of a Midland 4–2–2 at the head of a train of Midland stock, with an intrusive GWR Siphon at the head, crosses the viaduct on the MRC's 'Chiltern Green' exhibition layout.*

Below *A freight train heads out on the scenic section of Peter Denny's renowned 'Buckingham', one of the finest evocations of the steam age ever built.*

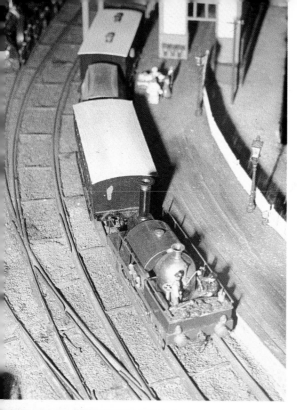

Left *Early days — part of Mike Sharman's eclectic 4mm scale layout depicting a typical single-sided broad gauge through station.*

Below *A former Stockton & Darlington 4–4–0 in light green at the head of a North Eastern passenger train passing across a small level crossing.*

Right *Light passenger working. Resplendent in the elaborate two-tone pre-1908 coach livery, a GWR steam railcar enters Botley Town, the Macclesfield club's fine 4mm scale exhibition layout. Note the cattle dock in the right foreground.*

Below right *Leslie Derbyshire has recreated the Kent & East Sussex, one of Colonel Stephen's light railways, in 4mm scale with his 'Maidstone Road' layout. In this shot we have an ex-LB&SCR 'Terrier' heading a train of two four-wheeled coaches.*

Above *The branch lines. 'Shallowford Park' is an excellent example of Southern Railway steam-age branch line modelling in 4mm scale.*

Left *Ex-NER 0–6–2T No 387 heads a passenger train on Alan Wright's 'Cheviotdale', a compact model of a North Eastern steam-age country branch station.*

Right *A mixed train on Martin Brent's 'Arcadia', a compact EM gauge layout built to explore new methods of construction before beginning work on a larger system.*

Above *Handling the goods. Brensham is typical of a steam-age station. The small goods yard is well filled with wagons, as would be the case in the mid-'30s. Note also the array of enamelled iron advertisements on the typical LMS diagonal slat fencing on E. Cox's 4mm scale model.*

Below *Leasingthorne is typical of the old North Eastern Railway, and featured the intensive coal traffic that was part and parcel of the steam-age railway.*

Above *A train of cattle wagons headed by a GWR 0–6–0 saddle tank passes through the Worcester Railway Modellers' Club model of Moreton-in-Marsh station.*

Below *A fine set of coal bins modelled in 4mm scale on R. Clarke's 'Westerham' layout.*

Above *On shed. GNR 2–4–0 on the turntable at 'Swaveney', a superb 4mm scale 18.83mm gauge exhibition layout representing the golden years at the turn of the century.*

Below *A typical small loco depot, with coal stage, water tank and crane, and shed.*

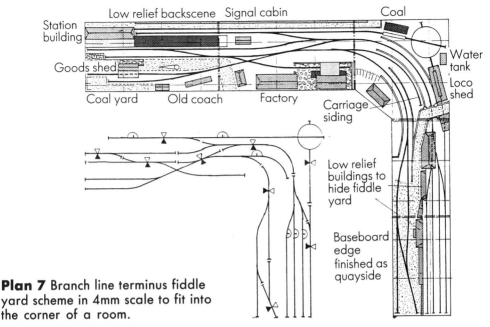

Station
building

Low relief backscene   Signal cabin   Coal

Goods shed

Coal yard   Old coach   Factory

Carriage
siding

Water
tank

Loco
shed

Low relief
buildings to
hide fiddle
yard

Baseboard
edge
finished as
quayside

Plan 7 Branch line terminus fiddle
yard scheme in 4mm scale to fit into
the corner of a room.

ner of a reasonably large room. As a
result, the fiddle yard is disguised by a
quayside setting which not only provides an opportunity for including some
interesting structures, but adds to the
shunting potential. It is important to appreciate that on this type of layout
almost all movement is shunting, and the
main line is a typical fisherman's walk,
three steps and overboard.

To add to the shunting movements,
there is a small factory, reached directly
from the run-round loop. There is also a
short carriage siding, enough to hold
two coaches comfortably, or three 50 ft
vehicles at a pinch.

Some of the scenic interest is given by
the multi-level setting in the corner. The
quayside line, quite reasonably, drops
on a fairly steep gradient whilst the small
loco depot is slightly raised.

The depot has a small turntable,
capable of handling a 4-4-0 or 2-6-0 as

well, of course, as 0-6-0 and 2-4-0 tender
locomotives. The loco shed has its track
extended through the scenic break and
descends, fairly steeply, to link into the
fiddle yard, enabling a little surreptitious
engine interchange. The multi-level arrangement adds to the overall effec-
tiveness of the scene.

The platform is kept short so that
there is room for locomotives to move
onto the depot even when a train oc-
cupies the bay road. This is a point that
needs to be carefully watched when using this particular arrangement of tracks,
as it is all too easy to end up with a bay
that can only be used on the rare occasions when one doesn't need to get a
loco onto or off the shed.

Figure 13 shows the way that the low-
relief quayside structures mask the fiddle yard. This, I think, is more effective
than a painted backscene. Similarly,
there is a small compressed road behind

Above *The loco shed at Hemyock on Maurice Deane's 00 gauge model of the Culm Valley branch. Built in the early '50s, this was one of the earliest models to be based, albeit loosely, on an actual prototype.*

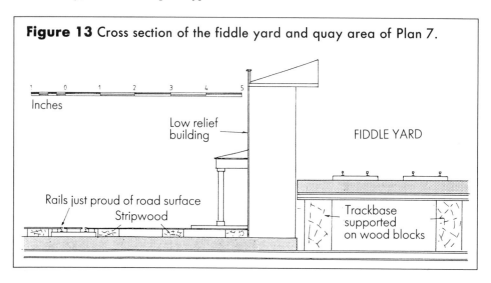

Figure 13 Cross section of the fiddle yard and quay area of Plan 7.

Inches

Low relief building

FIDDLE YARD

Rails just proud of road surface
Stripwood

Trackbase supported on wood blocks

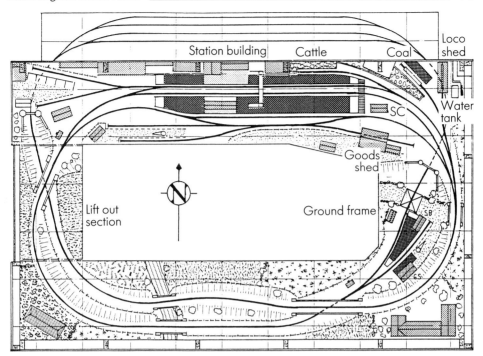

Plan 8 Branch line with a large passing station to fit into a 10 ft × 6 ft garden shed in 4mm scale.

the main station, with more low-relief modelling to create the illusion that the model serves a small town.

Although branch termini are justly popular, most branch stations were of the through pattern. Moreover, the cross-country line, which frequently had four-coach trains headed by medium-sized tender locomotives, didn't even have a terminus. In Plan 8 I give a scheme for just such a through station, located in a large garden shed. It's capacity is four- to five-coach trains.

The southern side is devoted to the main line, to give space in which you can see your trains moving through the model countryside. A small halt at the low level is provided to add both visual impact and to give a reason for running short trains. The gradients work out around 1 in 50, which means that your locomotives should have little difficulty in taking the maximum length train the loops can hold. Minimum radius is 24 in, and the entry points to the station loops are, I suggest, all large-radius curved turnouts, which look much better and improve the running.

The loops are situated outside the shed in a stout timber structure, which I show in cross section in Figure 14. The roof lifts to give access to the models, but is carefully made watertight. It would also be advisable to provide padlocks, and to ensure that this bulge is on the far side of the shed and not clearly

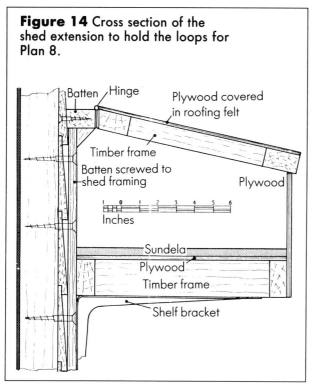

Figure 14 Cross section of the shed extension to hold the loops for Plan 8.

Batten / Hinge

Plywood covered in roofing felt

Timber frame

Batten screwed to shed framing

Plywood

```
1  0  1  2  3  4  5  6
```
Inches

Sundela

Plywood

Timber frame

Shelf bracket

Right *The Ventnor end of Shanklin, IOW, taken in the early '50s. However, only three items in this photo are wholly out of place in an Edwardian scene: the road sign against the bridge, the short skirts on the woman by the pram and, most of all, the ex-LSWR '02' on the train, for these locomotives did not reach the Island until the mid '20s.*

Plan 9 Elaborate branch line system to fit a space 15 ft × 8 ft in 4mm scale.

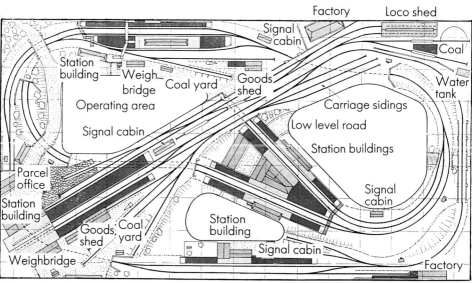

Factory　　　Loco shed

Signal cabin

Coal

Station building

Weigh bridge

Coal yard

Goods shed

Water tank

Operating area

Carriage sidings

Low level road

Station buildings

Signal cabin

Parcel office

Station building

Signal cabin

Goods shed

Coal yard

Station building

Weighbridge

Signal cabin

Factory

visible to anyone, since it is not exactly aesthetically pleasing.

The external loops will be invisible to the operator inside the shed and so it would, I think, be advisable to install some form of train detector. I have dealt with this in *The PSL Book of Model Railway Wiring*.

Given a moderately large area, a complete branch, with several stations, can be laid out, and providing one can give over a complete garage to the project, quite an interesting layout can result. Plan 9 shows what is possible in 4mm scale in such a space.

It is intended to be operated by the builder single-handedly, so the two main stations are located alongside one operating well. The smaller passing sta-

tion has only limited goods facilities and so can be treated simply as a passing point, whilst the junction has no goods sidings at all, serving solely as the entry to a large double track reverse loop. Although this arrangement can be criticized on strict prototype terms, since it is highly unlikely that two double track lines could converge into a single track bottleneck, the only reason I have shown the double track exposed is that I do not like covering more track than is strictly necessary, let alone introduce covered pointwork. In the odd-ball reality of the model world, this is, if you like, a bit of the adjacent double track main line.

The terminus is the main point of interest and I have taken advantage of the full length of a diagonal across the garage to lay it out with a prototypical sprawl. The loco shed is well away from the controls, hence I have opted for the simplest turntable arrangement, just one track entry, since it needs to be remotely controlled. The platforms can comfortably handle a four-coach train, and medium-sized tender locomotives would not be out of place.

If two operators are available, one can work the goods yard and the smaller passing station whilst the other handles the main and the three-road passing station. Three operators would lead to even more enjoyment.

I have not shown any hidden loops for the simple reason that, as drawn, the line can comfortably handle six or seven complete trains, with a fair amount of spare stock in the various sidings. Extra capacity could be arranged by introducing automatic control on the reverse loop to allow up to three trains to be stacked in each loop.

This layout will allow the introduction of the freight control system described in Chapter 20, and demonstrates the potential of the branch as an operating entity rather than a strictly scale scenic diversion.

Brixham was not typical of a GWR branch terminus, but reflected much of its origin as the independent Torbay & Brixham railway. The GWR platform awning is clearly a later addition.

CHAPTER 9
Light and industrial railways

Light railways were a small but fascinating part of the last period of the steam age railway scene, though a certain amount of misconception does exist. A light railway is not necessarily a lightly constructed line, but one authorized under the Light Railway Act of 1896 rather than by means of its own enabling Act. The purpose was to allow railways to be built to serve rural communities too small to attract the more expensive lines constructed under the old arrangement. The Act also empowered the Board of Trade to relax any or all of its regulations, which had the force of law on all conventional railways. This particular facility enabled the lines to dispense with full fencing, raised platforms and complex signalling and interlocking, usually on the condition that speeds were limited, generally to 25 mph. However, these relaxations were by no means automatic, and quite a few feeder lines were constructed by main-line railways using a Light Railway Order which were otherwise indistinguishable from branches built under a full Act of Parliament.

The Light Railway Act came far too late to any real effect on the railway system, and although several lines were built under its auspices, its main value lay in the obtaining of Light Railway Orders for existing lines to allow some relaxation of the onerous BoT regulations, which were drafted to cover main lines, and compelled railway companies to equip branch lines to carry the high-speed express trains they were quite incapable of handling. In recent years Light Railway Orders have also been used to allow preservation groups to take over various disused lines and re-open them for tourist traffic.

I've dwelt on the legal side of the Light Railways Act because it has, on many occasions, been used to excuse toylike practices on a model. Indeed, the late John Ahern, the man who did most to popularize the light railway theme, once remarked that it was a very good thing none of us had ever read the Act! Today, thanks largely to the fact that so many enthusiasts have been personally involved with preserved railways, more people are aware that there are limits to what a light railway can do — and remain legal.

The light railway model theme was very popular in the 1940s and '50s, largely as a direct result of the persuasive articles and photographs of John Ahern's

Left *Maurice Dean's earlier attempt at reproducing a prototype in little space involved this model of the Wantage terminus on the Wantage Tramway, a rare example of a roadside railway. Constructed immediately after the war, everything was scratchbuilt and the diminutive model of the line's Manning Wardle 0–4–0 tank No 7 was notable in its day, since there were no really small motors available and the model was literally built around a much modified Romford motor.*

Below left *A bevy of beauties on Ian Rice's 'East Suffolk Light'. Light railways can boast unconventional locomotives, acquired from goodness knows where. It is regarded as the height of bad taste to question their provenance!*

Plan 10 Light railway scheme for a space 10 ft × 8 ft in 4mm scale.

'Madder Valley Railway'. To a large extent the genre was swallowed by the branch line model, but there are many good reasons for choosing an independent light railway. Of these the best is that since most standard gauge light railways purchased their locomotives and stock from wherever they could, an heterogeneous collection of models can be readily justified. All you need do is to stick to small tank locomotives and short bogie or four-wheeled coaches and you'll not go far wrong.

Plan 10 depicts a light railway model set in a 10 ft × 8 ft room, with 24 in curves as a minimum. It is laid out for single-handed operation; the small passing station is merely a remotely controlled loop, though a little shunting can be carried out if someone is prepared to duck under the main baseboard. As was often the case with an independent light railway, the line is completely self-contained, but a link line to the adjacent main-line station is shown diving under the upper terminus where it ends in a simple fiddle yard. This would be used for stock transfer and exchange of goods wagons, for through passenger services were hardly ever arranged with the independent light railways. Indeed, even where a light railway was absorbed by a main-line company, or where the company used a Light Railway Order as a means of building a line, through services were virtually unknown, the passengers having to change trains at the junction.

With a self-contained layout of this nature, storage facilities become very important, since there is no handy fiddle yard where one can lose complete trains. Therefore two-road loco sheds are provided at each terminus and these, together with the coal stage road at the high level, provide storage for five locomotives, whilst a couple more can stand around in the yards. There is one carriage siding which will hold one set of coaches, while another set can stand in the main platform road of the high-level terminus. Spare goods vehicles will, of course, stand in the fiddle yard and I envisage a storage shelf below this so that stock can be swapped offstage. Traffic would consist of passenger services between the two termini with frequent deliveries of merchandise and despatch of agricultural produce from the various goods sidings.

I said earlier that a light railway was not necessarily lightly constructed. I want to go further, and say that most railways built under Light Railway Orders were, at the outset, well constructed and in excellent order. Many made use of short-lived materials such as timber, asbestos sheeting and corrugated iron in place of bricks and mortar, flimsier fencing and similar sensible economies. The track was invariably well laid and correctly aligned, though frequently in place of the traditional bullhead rail and chairs used for British steam age tracks, flat bottom rail spiked directly to the sleepers was employed and, in addition, the rails were frequently 40 or 50 lb section.

Where the light railway was part of a

main-line company, the infrastructure remained in good order right up to the end. The independent lines, most of which were one time or another part of the railway empire of Colonel H. F. Stephens, had to be run on a shoestring and, in places, it showed. I knew the Weston, Clevedon & Portishead Light Railway in the last year of its operating existence, and while it was undoubtedly run down and parts showed their age, the track was in reasonably good order to the very end and those locomotives in steam were as clean as any machines in the land. Unfortunately a lot of modellers, looking at photographs of these lines in their nadir, jumped to the conclusion that a light railway was a dilapidated railway and that as a result slap-happy workmanship can be the order of the day. In point of fact you need to take a good deal of care building a light railway, especially if you decide to emphasize the tight curves of the prototype and adopt 15 in radius for 00 gauge.

As I mentioned earlier, all preserved lines operate under Light Railway Orders and are excellent bases for a steam-worked model of the present day, the more so since large express classes are frequently to be seen working the trains. This is, of course, one prototype which can be studied in the field, but it must be realized that they are not in any way typical of the steam age proper – they are operated as tourist attractions, not as transport systems. This doesn't rule them out for modelling, but unfortunately the few examples I've seen of such models seem to exhibit all the least desirable features of the preserved railway in its early days, slapdash attention to detail and a generally amateurish look to the whole thing. This is, in my

Recent light railway modelling is typified by Martin Brent's 'Rye Harbour', an EM gauge layout based loosely on Kent & East Sussex practice, but operated as part of Southern region. The station was initially named Arcadia, but changed its name when the harbour extension was constructed.

SECR Class 'H' 0–4–4T in BR livery shunts at Rye Harbour, with a pair of SECR coaches in BR Southern green standing in the platform. The wagon is to be attached to the coaches, for most trains on the line were mixed. The combined passenger and goods train was mainly confined to light railways, where the rules were less stringent.

opinion, little short of an insult to the efforts of the devoted enthusiasts who have laboured hard and long to keep steam alive. A model preserved railway should be smart, neat and well ordered; there would just be rather more coaches, a lot more locomotives, far fewer goods vehicles and, above all, a great many more people about than one would expect on a true steam-age branch line.

The industrial railway was rarely a Light Railway, though it was almost always lightly constructed, often being laid more or less directly onto the existing ground, with only a bare minimum of essential earthworks. Such lines were very short lived and, if they left the owner's land, were constructed under wayleaves rather than the blessing of a government department. Their purpose was to exploit mineral resources, or to serve an industry.

A few industrial lines were very solidly constructed. There was, for example, a fine network of rail links in Trafford Park in Manchester. Many of the larger dock companies such as the Mersey Docks and Harbour Board and the Port of London Authority had extensive railways. Most large factories had rail networks, two of the better known being the lines at Cadbury's Bournville site and the Ford works in Dagenham. Many

collieries had their own railways as well.

There have been few models of such lines, the best known being perhaps Mike Sharman's multi-gauge works system which, in the '70s, was a popular feature of the exhibition circuit. It is a feature of the steam age which could be worth exploring, particularly now a number of kits are available for small industrial locomotives. This type of line has one great attraction for the enthusiastic modeller — anything goes! A disadvantage is that the tracks were very rough and derailments were by no means uncommon.

Part of Mike Sharman's mid-Victorian works scene, with tracks of three gauges in view, 7 ft broad gauge, standard gauge and narrow gauge. During its all too brief foray on the exhibition circuit this layout was always surrounded by fascinated viewers waiting anxiously to see what goodies would appear next. What is more to the point, everything worked!

CHAPTER 10
Choosing rolling-stock and gauges

Despite their importance in the scheme of things, locomotives, coaches and wagons are not physically connected to the layout, a point that becomes very obvious where portable layouts are involved. This has several important implications for any model railway. The most significant is that, whereas a fundamental error on the layout itself at the very least means an extensive reconstruction which can leave the layout inoperative, an absolutely unacceptable fault in a locomotive only means you have to remove the offending item and, hopefully, sell it to some less discerning individual. By unacceptable fault I mean not merely an out-of-proportion model, or one with some obvious inaccuracy, but one which, no matter how exquisite it may be when looked at in isolation, just doesn't happen to fit in with your overall scheme.

The practice of replacing earlier vehicles with later, better quality ones is of long standing and should, I think, be ingrained in every enthusiast's consciousness. There are a number of ready-to-run models on the market which are badly proportioned by today's high standards. They are, however, readily available and reasonably priced, virtues that are consistently undervalued by certain sections of the hobby. To paraphrase a popular proverb, an ill-proportioned working model on the layout is worth two true-to-scale masterpieces on the drawing board. The time to eliminate the not-quite-right locomotive, coach and wagon is when you have something better to put in its place.

The simple fact is that even if you have ample funds and can afford to commission near perfect models from the small, select band of professional model-makers who can make them for you, it will still be some time before you have anything to put on the layout. If you are building from a kit it can take a month or more to assemble the model correctly. If you decide to make a very accurate model of a specific locomotive, then the project can take anything from three months to a year. You can't do this and build a layout at the same time, and yet you can't test the reliability of your layout until you run trains over the tracks.

There is, therefore, a good, sensible reason for using, at the outset, a small selection of sound, commercial ready-to-run models to get the layout working. Indeed, in 4mm scale it is feasible to

A fine selection of modern ready-to-run 4mm scale locomotives on a layout built by Ron Riddles. This is the sort of collection most people begin with and which many retain as long as their interest remains in the hobby.

recreate an authentic BR scene of the 1950s and the LMS or GWR scene of the 1930s entirely from 4mm scale models you can buy from any well-stocked retailer, whilst for Southern or LNER modellers there is a smaller core of suitable models which, whilst not providing a completely comprehensive cover, do at least give one a flying start. After this, one may add kit-built or scratchbuilt models, hopefully of a steadily improving standard.

It is also possible to use stop-gap items, and this is very much the case where coaching stock is concerned. Clearly, this will only apply where the operation of the layout is of equal, if not greater, importance than the construction of the models themselves. I'm afraid that a lot of the emphasis on getting the locomotives and rolling-stock right from the outset comes from skilled model-makers who have little or no real interest in running them to timetable on a working layout. There is nothing wrong with this attitude, providing you appreciate that you are not a railway modeller, but a small scale locomotive or coach builder. In this case, I would suggest that unless you join a consortium which is engaged in constructing a high-class working layout in 4mm scale, you would be best advised to work in 7mm scale. The only serious objection to this size is the space you need for a working layout, but if you're not really bothered about this, it's an irrelevant factor. The question of cost in high quality locomotive and vehicle modelling is immaterial, since your main outlay will be on tools and time; in the former case, the cost is the same, while in the latter case, 7mm scale scratchbuilding is appreciably faster for the simple reason that the parts are not only larger but they're also easier to handle and fabricate and, above all, much easier to find when you drop them on the floor! However, the main advantage is that it is a great deal easier to appreciate quality workmanship in the larger scale.

However, throughout the following chapters I shall be mainly looking at the 4mm scale scene. There are two reasons, the first of which is immediately apparent to anyone who has ever been to a model railway exhibition — 4mm scale predominates throughout the hobby. As a result, the largest selection of ready-to-run models and kits is for 4mm scale. There is, however, one important point to consider regarding the three gauges, 00, EM and P4. There are many arguments concerning these, all of which seem to revolve around the concept that 'scale is good, therefore the closer to scale the better', but there are other considerations.

The first is the layout itself. As I hope I have shown in the previous chapters, there is absolutely no chance of producing a true-to-scale model of a large and interesting station in 4mm scale in the normal home. In particular, true-to-scale track radii are next door to impossible. Regrettably, P4 stock is not noted for its ability to negotiate sharp curves and, to my way of thinking, a 4mm scale model locomotive which flatly refuses to go round the curves of a normal layout is a flawed model. It is all very well raving about its fidelity to its full-sized original; the plain fact is that it fails in the prime test of the prototype, the ability to haul a payload over the railway! 00 and, to a very considerable extent, EM gauge models will negotiate the tight corners which are regrettably essential on a working layout, and if you don't want a working layout what on earth are you doing in 4mm scale to begin with?

There is also the question of convenience. Thirty years ago, when one either scratchbuilt or used the newfangled loco kits, there was little bother in adopting any scale gauge combination that caught your fancy. Today, the situation is radically different, since with the excellent ready-to-run models now on the market, one can get off to a flying start. All these models are built to run on 16.5 mm 00 gauge track, and whilst conversion to EM is fairly straightforward, modification to P4 seems to be extreme-

As a complete contrast, here we have 7mm scale scratch-built LNER (Great Northern section) stock built by Geoff Bigmore.

ly complicated since received wisdom maintains that a fully compensated chassis is essential and that the rigid frames of the ready-to-run model are unacceptable. Of course, it could well be that the P4 protagonists have a strong masochistic streak and revel in creating unnecessary difficulties for themselves, as I have seen rigid-framed P4 models run perfectly well.

However, an important point to bear in mind is that although we are aware that 16.5mm only represents 4 ft 1½ in in 4mm scale, on the overwhelming majority of 00 gauge layouts it still remains the most accurate measurement around the track! If the main object is intensive operation, then I consider that it would, today, be a serious error to choose other

than 16.5mm gauge for 4mm scale, whilst, as I've indicated earlier, I consider that, where accurate models of locomotives, coaches and wagons are of paramount interest, 7mm scale has most of the advantages. An important consideration is that whereas a top class scratchbuilt EM or P4 locomotive has a very poor resale value (less, in practice, than an equivalent 00 model), a 7mm scale model of equal quality could fetch a handsome four-figure price at auction. Whilst this is of little immediate interest to a modeller, it not only makes one's estate more valuable, but it means that, if times are hard, the sale of only one locomotive may well stave off one's creditors for long enough to give time to re-organize one's affairs.

More scratchbuilding, a superb NER 0–6–0 on the 'Leasingthorne' layout.

CHAPTER 11
Locomotives

The locomotive must always be the centrepiece of the steam age model railway and might, therefore, appear to need the most space in this book. Indeed, were I merely to set out all I consider of interest on this one subject, I could easily fill two books this size — and still leave out things you might think far more important. Instead, I'm making one basic assumption, that you not only know something about steam locomotives, but you also have a number of favourite designs. Clearly, the layout you build should be capable of displaying these in an appropriate setting.

This can cause a few problems, for if you happen to want to run a model of Stephenson's *Rocket* alongside a LNWR 'George the Fifth', you'll meet pedantic individuals who will point out how impossible it is. However, I think you may also find a few who happen to know that a photograph exists showing the two together, *Rocket* being a replica, of course. Which is why I chose that particular pair of machines...

There is nothing wrong with an eclectic collection of models; I've known a few such layouts in my time and, without exception, they were good fun. If, on the other hand, you want greater realism, then you need to be a trifle selective. This is not without its side benefits, as it can reduce what could otherwise be an unmanageably large and costly collection to a more practical size. Indeed, as I see it, the only sensible reason for being selective as to prototype is to eliminate the other attractive locomotives. I'm afraid that I often echo MacHeath and murmur, 'How happy would I be with either, were t'other fair charmer away!'

There is no great problem discovering what locomotives went where and precisely how they appeared at any given moment in time. Dozens of detailed locomotive studies have been published, and drawings of most classes have appeared. Much more to the point, a very wide range of kits exists in 4mm scale to supplement the quite large range of ready-to-run models. Indeed, it is all too easy to end up with a heterogeneous collection of locomotives, so I would suggest that some overall plan should be drawn up. This is particularly the case if your intention is to operate the layout in accordance with prototype practice, since, unlike the modern diesel or electric locomotive, which can tackle almost any type of traffic, steam locomotives

Type	Period 1 1890–1914	Period 2 1915–1930	Period 3 1930–1960
Express passenger	2-2-2, 4-2-2, 2-4-0, 4-4-0	2-4-0, 4-4-0, 4-4-2, 4-6-0	4-6-0, 4-6-2
Mixed traffic	0-6-0, 2-4-0, 0-4-2	0-6-0, 2-6-0, 4-4-0	2-6-0, 4-6-0
Heavy freight	0-6-0, 0-8-0	0-6-0, 0-8-0, 2-8-0	2-8-0, 2-10-0
Freight	0-6-0	0-6-0	0-6-0, 2-6-0
Large tank	0-6-0T	2-6-2T	2-6-2T, 2-6-4T
Small tank	0-6-0T, 2-4-0T, 0-4-2T	0-6-0T, 0-4-4T, 0-6-2T, 2-6-2T	0-6-0T, 0-6-2T, 2-6-2T

Note Before 1890, the overwhelming majority of locomotives in Britain had only six wheels.

were fitted to their duties. Quite apart from the size of the boiler and the number and size of the cylinders, the diameter of the wheels and their arrangement was of significance. The table above provides a generalized guide to the types used in the heyday of steam.

This table must be taken solely as a general guide rather than a rigid set of rules, for quite apart from the fact that many old classes lasted a very long time, the practice of individual companies varied. In particular, the LNER used 4-6-2s during the 1920s, whilst the GWR scrapped its only 'Pacific' at the same time. The Southern didn't acquire 'Pacifics' until 1940 but built the very late 'Schools' Class 4-4-0 as a major express class.

Then there were the oddities. The Great North of Scotland became convinced that the 4-4-0 was the best answer to all its traffic needs, whilst the LT&SR remained faithful to its distinctive 4-4-2 tanks until the last years of its independent existence. There were, furthermore, many areas where 0-6-0s did virtually all the work.

One important point to remember is the existence of joint lines and running powers. This meant that locomotives from two or even three companies might be seen at one station. The record was set, in pre-group days, by Carlisle

Citadel, which has led to several models being based on this very impressive station. In the group provincial era, Oxford took the crown, where the GWR and LMS had their own stations, but LNER and, surprisingly, even Southern locomotives put in guest appearances. Furthermore, in the London area there are several locations where a small stretching of probabilities would permit the construction of a precursor of the current Thameslink services, provided it is appreciated that the Metropolitan or District railways would also be involved.

Selecting locomotives you might like to own is one thing, but owning them is something else. There are three main ways of acquiring a model locomotive: buying it ready-to-run, building it from a kit or scratchbuilding. Let's look at each in turn.

Buying ready-to-run models does seem to limit the choice, in today's world, to 00 or N gauge models. Certainly, when you look at the advertisements in the major magazines, that is the immediate impression and this is where you tend to begin. In 4mm scale the selection is reasonable: the GWR and LMS are well represented, there is a small selection of BR designs and, as the older company classes are generally available in BR livery, it is not too difficult to set up a model based on British Railways, or

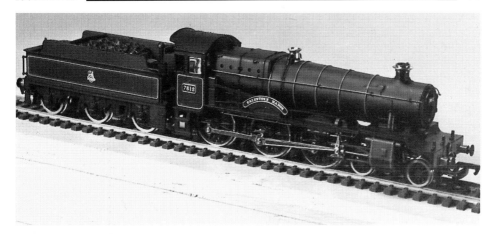

Top *A ready-to-run GWR 'Manor' in 00, initially from the Mainline stable.*

Above *When Hornby introduced a series of pre-nationalization 4–4–0s, in 00 gauge, they elected to give their GWR 'County' Class the same name as the old 0 gauge No 2 Special* County of Bedford.

the LMS or GWR in the '30s. The LNER is not too badly served, but the Southern is very patchy. In N gauge the coverage is very similar, though the choice is not quite so large.

The advantage of a ready-to-run model is, first and foremost, that it is there. It is also reasonably priced and so it does make, in 4mm scale and N gauge, a good starting point, unless you happen to want to model, shall we say, the LNWR around 1910, in which case you

are, apparently, stymied.

This isn't necessarily the case. I chose LNWR 1910 because an influential writer of the 1930s, S.R. Loxton, made just that choice. Moreover, he wasn't prepared to build his own locomotives, but he was prepared to order them from a specialist manufacturer. He had a few problems, which he related in an article in 1940, but that's by the way. The point is that there are a number of individual craftsmen who will, for a price, build you any loco, or assemble any kit you care to mention. It costs, but if you must have a particular machine, then it is a feasible route. Be prepared to wait a year or more for your model.

In addition, there is a good second-hand market, and some retailers are able to offer a selection of ready-made models of unusual prototypes. There are two advantages: you get to see the model and, ideally, check that it works before you hand over your money. There are also offers in small advertisements from individual modellers in the magazines; there is a little risk you might get a poor model, but there is a larger probability that someone will beat you to it.

As you are probably aware, no class of locomotive was at all homogeneous, quite apart from the almost inevitable differences as each successive batch went through the shops, and rebuilds, modifications and even, on some occasions, the aftermath of an accident led to each machine taking on a character of its own. The normal ready-to-run loco can be a fairly general model; most of the Hornby range are typical of the class as a whole, whereas several of the former Mainline models were very accurate replicas of a particular preserved machine.

It is possible to customize the model to fit your own requirements. Changing the number, and where appropriate, the name is a common and fairly straightforward matter. Etched replicas of prototype nameplates are available, and, where appropriate, numbers and smokebox plates as well. These are far superior to the printed version normally supplied on the boxed model. Transfers for cabside numbers and for tender or tank insignia are also available, and mat-

ched paint for virtually every livery style that ever existed can be bought.

Packs of detailing parts are available for most ready-to-run locomotives. In addition, kits have been produced to transform a locomotive into another class that is substantially similar in basic outline, though different in detail. It is even possible to buy etched chassis kits for most ready-to-run 4mm scale locomotives, and these are particularly useful where it is intended to convert the model to run on 18.2mm (EM) or 18.83mm (P4) gauge tracks. However, I am a trifle dubious of the wisdom of much of this, since it seems to me that one is doing a great deal of work on a model that is reasonably satisfactory as it is, reducing its resale value as you go along.

As an alternative, there are complete loco kits. Unfortunately, there are loco kits and loco kits and whereas some are a pleasure to put together, others are absolute pigs. There is also a more significant consideration, that although many classes are listed, there is no absolute guarantee that, at any one moment in time, the precise kit you want is actually available.

There are two main types of loco kits: cast white metal and etched brass. The distinction can be a little fuzzy, since more and more white metal kits include a selection of etchings, whilst most etched kits have a proportion of their parts cast in white metal; it is a trifle difficult to etch a dome, chimney or safety valve.

One of the hazards of kit construction is the instruction sheet. Whilst I have had little difficulty, this is due to the fact that, having a sound engineering background, a good deal of experience and, above all, having made a start with scratchbuilding, I can put the majority of

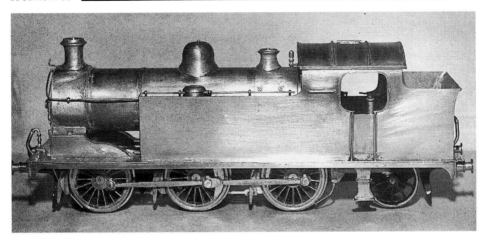

Glasgow & South Western 0–6–2T in 4mm scale, built from an etched brass kit.

kits together without any instructions. In fact, I often depart deliberately from the script because I think my way is better. I mention this, not as a boast, but as a warning, for if you seek the advice of an experienced kit builder you may well be told his way of doing things, which might not be a good idea for you.

Many kits are provided with alternative parts and fittings, allowing the builder to make the specific sub-class he prefers. In my opinion it is probably easier to make these changes whilst assembling a locomotive than to carve and cut an existing locomotive unless the types are very similar indeed.

However, it is possible to do so much fitting work on a kit that one virtually ends up scratchbuilding the model at greater expense. A good deal of mystique has grown up around scratchbuilding; there is a firm belief that one requires extraordinary skill and endless patience, whereas all you really need is a good deal of determination and a selection of respectable tools. Of course, an

extensive workshop does make things fractionally easier, but many excellent models have been built with a rudimentary set-up.

There are three enormous advantages to scratchbuilding. The first is that, providing you can collect enough information, you can have any prototype you like. The second is that it is far and away cheaper than building a kit and, in some cases, cheaper than a ready-to-run model as well. The most important advantage of all is that you have the supreme satisfaction of knowing that it is all your own work.

Unfortunately, the supply of kits in 4mm scale is such that, unless your period is before 1900, you are likely to have your model matched by a commercial product, which is decidedly annoying. However, when scratchbuilding you are not confined to any specific scale. More and more modellers are rediscovering the virtues of 7mm scale as a field for the scratchbuilder.

There is, for a start, little need to com-

A partly completed model, by Alan Cruickshank, of a Metropolitan 4–4–0 in the rare 3/16in scale, S gauge. In his scale you either make it yourself or go without!

promise on matters of detail. Modern motors enable a powerful power unit to be almost completely hidden within the firebox, allowing for such intriguing features as full internal motion. Opening smokebox doors, revealing the tube-plate, blastpipe and, where appropriate, superheater header, are perfectly practical fittings, whilst full cab detail is almost obligatory. Yet little of this fascinating detail work is so small as to strain the eyesight of either the builder or the viewer.

In addition, the final product is much more rugged. This shows up not only in a greater strength of small parts, but also applies in considerable force to the chassis and motor drive. It is much easier to arrange for sound mechanical arrangements when you have nearly four times as much room to dispose the components and, with the far greater inertia of the much more massive model, the running qualities of an 0 gauge model are considerably enhanced. One side effect of this is that, paradoxically, it is rather more suited to compact layouts than the smaller scales, since the operator has far better control of the models and can carry out the necessary shunting movements with greater precision.

Above *This Midland 0–4–4T was lovingly scratchbuilt in 2mm scale by Tim Watson. Despite its diminutive size, it is fully detailed and runs superbly.*

Below *A lovely model of British Railways Standard Class '7' 'Pacific',* Black Prince.

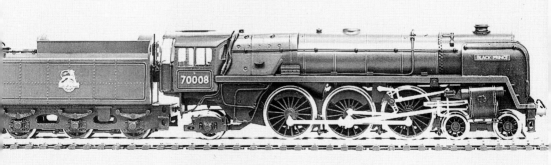

CHAPTER 12
On shed

The steam locomotive was a rugged beast and kept on running regardless; all it needed was a good clout with a hammer in the right place now and then. That, in outline, is the common belief among enthusiasts. In point of fact it is the supposedly delicate, intricate diesel locomotive that is the rugged, reliable beast, beaten only by the simple, nothing-much-to-go-wrong electric locomotive. In contrast, the steam locomotive was a temperamental machine that wanted humouring at all times and needed to be thoroughly cleaned out at frequent intervals if it was to keep going at all.

This is why there were so many loco sheds dotted about the system. These were not nice comfortable places to house the machines overnight, but were provided as much to give the fitters somewhere to tackle the routine maintenance needed to keep the beasts working. A shed was liberally provided with inspection pits, partly to allow the enginemen to oil the internal parts but mainly to give good access to the works for maintenance.

Apart from the regular tinkering with the works, there was a daily routine that had to be carried out. At the outset, the boiler water level needed to be topped up, the fire had to be lit and steam raised. This was a slow process and so, on shed, this job was carried out by the firelighter rather than the engine crew. It is probable that few readers under 50 have ever had to light a coal fire in a grate, let alone in a firebox. It is not an easy task, even with split railway sleepers, soaked in creosote and therefore highly flammable, to help. It took a good deal of judgement to decide when to add coal to the blaze — too soon and you put out the fire, too late and the kindling burned through before the coal lit. It was a lot easier, if more hazardous, to collect a shovel full of burning coals from another locomotive, or, frequently, a small furnace built for this purpose, and use that as the core of the fire.

When the fire was well alight and the pressure gauge moving steadily around the dial, the crew would book on and read the notices which told them of any special features to watch out for, temporary speed restrictions and the like. Then, collecting their tools and oil, they would set about checking the locomotive. Every oil box on the locomotive had to be filled, the condition of the lamps checked and the wicks in the lubricators trimmed, and then, when full boiler pressure had been reached, they could set off on their day's work — assuming that the bunker and water tanks had been filled at the end of the previous shift.

In general, the bunker held enough coal for a full shift, but the water would need to be replenished at frequent intervals. On local runs, this was done at strategically located water cranes, either at the end of a journey or, occasionally, during a specially lengthened wait. The water crane ended in a leather hose which was placed into the tank and was fed from a large capacity high-level tank through a large diameter pipe. Several thousand gallons could be delivered in

minutes and the man on the valve needed to be sharp if the tank wasn't to overfill.

On long-distance runs, water troughs were provided. These enabled a locomotive to replenish the tender on the run; once again, it called for a good deal of skill to do the job properly. It was essential to take on enough water to carry the train through to the next set of troughs, but, on the other hand, if the tank overflowed it was all Lombard Street to a China orange that the surplus would end up in the leading coach. This was one reason why most express trains had a van at the front!

At the end of a shift, the fireman, usually with some help from the driver,

The loco facilities at Kingswear, *a standard GWR turntable with a couple of spurs off. Note the pit and water crane in the foreground.*

4mm scale scratchbuilding at its best — a superb 4mm scale P4 gauge model of a GNR Stirling single. Note how the coal in the tender is well down, as the loco has just come off its run.

would have shovelled up to eight tons of coal into the firebox and, in the process, moved nearer 12 tons, since it was necessary on most locomotives to trim the bunker from time to time, in other words, to get back into the tender and shovel the coal forward. This brings us to the first detail that actually affects a model, the level of coal in the bunker.

Most models are shown with full bunkers. Occasionally, as in the case of tender-drive locomotives, this is inevitable in order to hide the motor. More often it is not, and the sensible modeller will depict most of his stud in an intermediate condition, with the bunker well depleted but enough coal left to give the impression that there is no risk of running short before the day's

work is over.

Only a portion of coal is flammable; depending on the grade it has a proportion of ash and clinker. This ends up in three places. The larger unburnable material remains on the firegrate, and has to be knocked out and broken up before it clogs the fire. Hence, each locomotive was provided with a rake and a pricker, long steel bars which were pushed into the fire to stir the incandescent firebed about and, hopefully, get most of the clinker down into the ashpan. A proportion of the unburned material would be small enough to fall down with the vibration of the locomotive, but the finest ash was drawn through the fire tubes by the force of the blast. Much of this shot clear out of the chimney and fell on the lineside, but a fair proportion ended in the smokebox as char.

As the shift wore on, the level of ash in the ashpan rose steadily. Unfortunately, the primary air for the fire had to go over the ashpan and, towards the end of a long hard run, the supply of air would be throttled, often leading to a marked drop in performance. Likewise, as char built up in the smokebox it covered the lower fire tubes. Ash could build up inside the tubes as well, and in extreme cases, the evaporation rate fell off to such an extent that the locomotive lost power. This was more common in winter, when the boiler also had to provide steam for carriage heating, and it was by no means uncommon for the train heating to be shut off when the boiler was playing up!

At the end of the shift, all this rubbish had to be cleared out. It was a rotten job, as most of the ash and all of the char had to be shovelled out by hand. The tubes needed to be blown out with a jet; the favourite method was to use a steam lance, a long tube with a valve at the back end, coupled to the boiler by a flexible pressure hose. It got rather hot! All this was done over the ashpit, a fairly deep hole between the tracks into which most of the ash was pushed. Later, it had to be shovelled out, and few sheds were provided with mechanical hoists to load the ash into wagons.

Once the waste from the shift had been removed, the locomotive would be coaled and watered. Coaling was carried out in three distinct ways. The simplest was to fill the bunker by hand, using small skips which could be manhandled and emptied over the side. In many cases a small crane was provided, generally manually worked, but oc-

casionally powered.

The next pattern of coal stage was the raised tippler, which was provided at larger sheds. Coal wagons were pushed up a steep ramp and the coal shovelled into small barrows on short rails. These

The ash plant at Ashton MPD, LMS. The ash was shovelled into the skip, which dumped it into the waiting wagon.

Above *A primitive coaling stage under construction. The crane is based on an early GWR design and the brick-built structure is typical. The coal is real!*

Left *The coal hopper at Ashton MPD. The wagon is on its way up to be turned over at the top and its contents dropped into the stage.*

Above right *The turntable on Mac Pyrke's 00 gauge 'Berrow' branch.*

were then emptied into the waiting locomotives. This type of coal stage had one great advantage, that the shed foreman could see that the top link locomotives got the best coal, and the poorer grades could be worked out on less important duties where there would be a chance for the crew to pull the fire round whilst standing at a station or signal.

The final pattern was the large overhead hopper, where coal was tipped into the top by the wagon load and dropped out of the bottom into the bunkers. On the face of it, this was highly efficient; it needed the minimum of hands, it filled the tenders very quickly and assisted a quick turn-round. Unfortunately it not only mixed good coal with indifferent stuff, but also broke the larger lumps down into small stuff. Indeed, one reason the GWR avoided this type of bunker was that the Welsh steam coal used by that company was extreme-

ly brittle and even more likely to end up as indifferent dust if dropped into the tender from a great height. Working coal hoists are a feature one may add to a model scene. I've seen several designs on paper, but I can't recall ever seeing one actually work.

With the exception of some very small sheds, and others in areas such as South Wales where tank engines did most of the work, all sheds had a turntable. Most were of the well pattern, where a large circular hole held a table with its girders underneath, mounted at 4 ft 9 in centres so that the rails bore directly on their supports. The GWR, always the odd man out, favoured a shallower pattern with the girders outside the tracks. Some well-type tables, particularly those in roundhouse sheds and close to major stations, had light frames inside the well which carried planking to avoid the risk of accidents to shed staff.

The earliest tables were so small that

locomotives had to be detached from their tenders before turning, but by 1860 the decks were long enough to take the short machines of their day, usually something between 45 ft and 55 ft in diameter. As locomotive lengths increased, the tables needed lengthening, and here the GWR pattern table scored since it proved possible to add an extra few feet with outriggers. This increase in length caused a good deal of friction between the mechanical and civil engineering departments, and in one case precipitated a tremendous row when the CME ordered a new table without bothering to inform the Chief Engineer beforehand.

There are not many commercial turntables on the market, and the few really good ones cost as much as a top quality mass-produced locomotive. The working ones are invariably large enough to handle the biggest models on the market, which is fine for the main-line model of the '30s or later. Branch lines and period models need something smaller — a 50 ft to 60 ft table is about right, and scratchbuilding seems the most obvious answer. Whilst the organization of a fully mechanized table calls for a good deal of time, effort and not a little skill and ingenuity, there are two alternatives. One is a forefinger placed against the side of the table, and the other is a worm drive under the baseboard leading to a handle on the side of the baseboard. As a slight refinement, this worm drive can be powered by a redundant locomotive mechanism; any motor drive requires at least a 500:1 reduction, and two locomotive worm drives will generally provide 900:1.

An extensive — by model standards — 00 gauge loco depot on Ron Riddle's 4mm scale layout.

CHAPTER 13
Coaches

The steam age saw the railway coach develop from crude beginnings to a highly sophisticated vehicle and, as with locomotives, a great deal depends on the period one is attempting to model. Although the compartment coach, with or without a side gangway, predominated throughout the steam age, there were plenty of examples of saloon coaches around. Indeed, one good reason for setting one's period before 1900 is the incredible degree of variation that existed in coach designs during the Victorian period. It was not until the 1890s that the typical British compartment coach became so firmly established.

From the outset, coaches were built on separate underframes. Initially these were timber baulks, but before long iron girders became increasingly popular, not merely because they were stronger, but also because there was no longer a limit on length. Until the middle of the nineteenth century, the majority of coaches had four wheels. From around 1850 onwards, six-wheeled stock came into favour until the bogie coach arrived around 1890. Needless to say there was a considerable overlap, the final four-wheelers coming out of service in BR days, though six-wheeled stock had virtually disappeared by the '30s.

The BR Mk1 coach which first appeared in the early '50s was quite revolutionary in design, since the underframe became part of the body shell with the result that the familiar solebars disappeared and were replaced by a central spine. These coaches were the last of the steam age vehicles and are readily available in both 4mm scale and N gauge in a selection of basic versions. The prototype had an extensive range of variations on a standard theme and has been the subject of a detailed study. As the body shells and windows were standardized, plastic Mk1 coaches can be suitably doctored to produce the major variants within the fleet.

The grouped era is also provided for in 4mm scale ready-assembled stock. GWR prototypes are fairly well covered for a 1930s theme, though the standard trick of offering a brake 3rd and composite coach came unstuck when the Airfix 'Centenary' coaches were produced to this theme, since this gave an unduly high proportion of first class accommodation in the train. In any case, the 'Centenary' stock was very limited in usage, and the Collett corridor stock in-

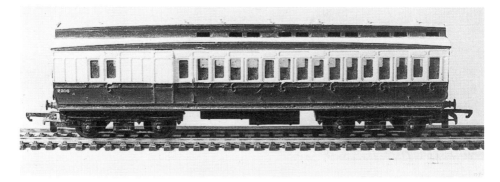

Top *Ripe for conversion, the Hornby (ex-Triang) non-corridor clerestory brake third coach.*

Above *The Hornby composite clerestory coach. These are the original versions featuring the early bogie with open axleboxes and very grim wheels.*

Below *Ex-LT&SR non-corridor stock at Barking in 1951. The similarity between these bodies and the Hornby short clerestory stock is quite marked.*

itially produced by Mainline is more representative of the late '30s. The earlier coaches, produced by Hornby, are a trifle out of proportion. For local working, the B set is reasonably useful whilst the trailer car is as much at home on the main line as it is on the archetypal branch.

The LMS has ex-Airfix stock, both corridor and non-corridor, which provides a good basis, whilst the earlier panelled ex-Mainline stock is useful to add variety to a rake. The Hornby LMS coach is probably the most accurate of its grouped stock. LNER and Southern are provided by Hornby; the LNER stock is well proportioned, but the Southern coaches are merely the GWR shells in green. In addition, Hornby has produced two sets of GWR clerestory roofed stock. The later corridor vehicles, though lacking in panelling, are accurate models, but the earlier non-corridor coaches, now re-introduced and, at the time of writing, produced in LMS colours, are more correctly a typical turn-of-the-century 50 ft bogie coach. Although fitted with

clerestory roofs, the body shells have a three-arc profile and provide a convenient basis for turn-of-the-century stock.

When one turns to kits, a far wider selection is available. There are two basic forms of kit on the market, in plastic and etched brass. Older wooden and card kits can, I think, be safely discounted today, but a brief mention should be made of the PC series which had pre-printed acetate sides and, whilst difficult to assemble properly, certainly cut out what is far and away the most difficult part of the coach modeller's craft.

The etched brass kits represent the top end of the market, being accurate, well detailed and nowhere near as difficult to assemble as many people believe. Indeed, the great advantage of the etched brass kit is that you do have a second chance, as the kit can be reduced to its component parts by heating the lot on a sheet of aluminium over a hotplate and teasing the sections apart with tweezers. However, it is essential to paint the bodies after assembly.

The range of plastic coach kits is hap-

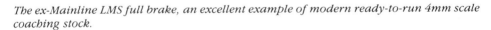

The ex-Mainline LMS full brake, an excellent example of modern ready-to-run 4mm scale coaching stock.

A LSWR 56 ft non-corridor full third, a superior model made from etched frets.

pily increasing, with an emphasis on the grouped era. With these kits, it is a good idea to paint the sides before assembly, as it is much easier to do whilst the whole unit is flat. It also permits the adding of the windows at an early stage; painting a 4mm scale coach with windows in place is not an easy task. In my experience, a coach is far more difficult to paint well than a locomotive; the area involved is larger and there is less opportunity for hiding sloppy workmanship. For my part, I would never consider anything other than an airbrush for this purpose, by which means it is relatively easy to arrive at the smooth uniform finish required.

Whether one is considering the early wooden-bodied stock, the modern all-steel vehicles or the intermediate composite bodies, with steel panels on wooden frames, one important design feature is common to all. The window and door openings are standardized, as is the cross section of the body. This is implicit in the prototype manufacturing methods.

These methods gave the coach designers a fairly free hand. The old wooden bodies were built up from a large number of standard frames, initially cut by hand but, as technology improved, by machines. In effect, they were built from kits of parts. Even when all-steel construction was introduced, the principle of part standardization was maintained, with the result that a wide variety of arrangements were possible in a standard body shell and full advantage was taken of the fact. The full potential of this can best be studied in the BR Mk1 coach, which had one of the longest, and certainly the largest, production runs of any British coach design.

This part standardization can make the modelmaker's work a lot easier. For a start, plastic coaches offer enormous potential for modification, since it is a matter of cutting, carving and reassembling the parts into a new design. The usual advice suggests that one should study the prototype carefully and plan the operation in every detail before starting out. I am not wholly convinced that this is the best approach, and my advice is to take a slightly battered coach body, a razor saw, a small steel square and start hacking. Whilst it sounds easy to slice a plastic coach into sections and stick them back together in a different order, the technique of making a true square cut and then getting the parts together so that, at the end of the day, the joins are invisible is a fairly skilled one.

Skills are acquired, not inborn, and one's 'prentice efforts are generally unsatisfactory. Happily, at most model railway exhibitions, one will find a stall selling members' unwanted equipment. In most cases there are odd coach bodies, minus parts, cracked, broken and in a pretty poor state, going for quite modest sums. In addition, many coach kit manufacturers have boxes of production rejects on sale at greatly reduced prices. You may even have some unwanted old coaches yourself. These are good practice material, and indeed I know quite a few modellers who regard them as their main source of materials for their coach fleet.

There are a couple of points to watch. The first and most important is that all cuts must be square and true. It is no use trusting to your eye — you must use a guide of some sort to ensure that the saw doesn't wander. Then you have to remember that the saw removes a definite amount of material at each cut. You can allow for this when deciding where to cut, or you can use a sliver of styrene sheet as a filler.

When assembling the parts, it is essential to keep them correctly aligned whilst the cement is hardening. Here, a simple plywood jig makes life that much easier. Indeed, it can be worth making several such jigs so that you can work on a number of coaches at once. Although plastic cements set fairly quickly, the joints remain soft for several hours and it is good practice, once you are certain they are correctly aligned, to let the sides harden overnight before moving on to the next stage. It is usually necessary to reinforce the joins on the inside with small patches of styrene sheet.

Once the sides are hard, the joins need disguising. For this reason the ideal place to make a cut is along the side of a door, but this isn't always practical. Providing the joins were well made, there will only be a small scar, and a little careful work with fine wet-and-dry abrasive paper

Martin Brent took two Lima four-wheeled bodies and joined them to form a freelance light railway coach, reminiscent of the saloon stock formerly running on the Weston, Clevedon & Portishead Railway.

will generally provide a smooth finish. Where flush-sided coaches are concerned, it is a good idea to rub down the entire side to produce a uniform finish.

Unwanted window apertures can be filled with plastic inserts. These need to be very carefully smoothed down. Smaller holes can be filled with a suitable plastic putty; the two-part epoxy fillers sold for car repairs are, I find, very suitable for this purpose. As before, careful smoothing down is essential.

In many cases, you will need to provide a new underframe, and 3mm ply is suitable for this. It is usually possible to re-use the original roof, but it needs a good deal of attention since the moulded ventilators will inevitably be in the wrong place. The most satisfactory solution is to file the old projections away and produce a perfectly smooth roof profile with wet-and-dry paper. Then the positions of the roof vents can be

carefully marked out with a small prick from a scriber and holes drilled to take commercial cast or moulded vents of the correct pattern. Rain strips are easily made from thin plastic rod, cemented in place with plastic solvent.

Alternatively, it is not too difficult to produce new roofs. You need first of all to make a wooden profile, and this, whilst taking quite a while, is a job that only needs doing the once for a particular pattern of coach design. Then, with the aid of heat, 20 thou styrene sheet is moulded to the correct profile to form a new roof. It is possible to do this by laying a sheet of plastic over the former, placing both on a metal tray and then putting the lot into a warm oven. I prefer to use a hair dryer on the workbench; it may take a shade longer, but not only is the process under control, it also saves a good deal of family argument as well.

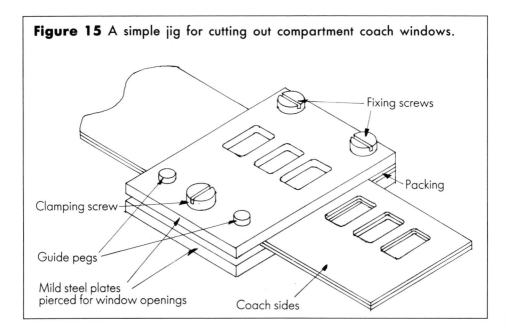

Figure 15 A simple jig for cutting out compartment coach windows.

Fixing screws

Packing

Clamping screw

Guide pegs

Mild steel plates pierced for window openings

Coach sides

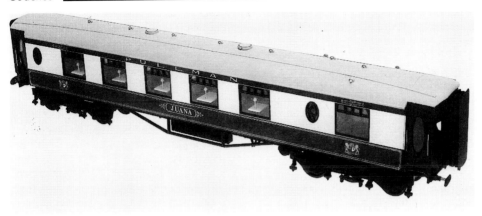

The ultimate in steam age luxury, a fine model of first class Pullman car 'Juana'.

The modular design of coach bodies makes it a relatively straightforward matter to organize body shell production at home, since a number of units will be built to a uniform design. Hence templates to determine the curve of the roof, the tumblehome of the body sides and, above all, the cross section of the coach body, are well worth making. The most important tool is the window-cutting jig, shown in Figure 15. The idea is to position this over a pre-cut strip of material and then cut the windows out by any convenient means. The tool is made from thin sheet steel, which is adequate for a normal home run of, at the most, 12 coaches to one design. Case hardening might be worthwhile if one is used to the technique. Clearly, the template holes need to be very accurately cut, but they need not be precisely to scale. The object is to ensure that all windows are of uniform size and in line, since any divergence will be very noticeable along the coach body.

The sides can be cut from 1mm ply or styrene sheet. In the latter case it is feasi-ble to make up the body from several layers of sheet, leaving a gap between the inner and outer sides for glazing material. Whilst this appears to involve a little more work, the fact that many steam age coaches have identical windows on either side makes it feasible to run four sheets of thin plastic through the jig at once.

The raised beading for the older panelled coaches can be cut from a single sheet of plastic, but on the whole I consider that the older method of applying strips of thin material, simulating the prototype beading, is easier.

Grab handles are bent from brass wire — picture wire is a convenient source. The 'T' handles for doors can be made from a brass gimp pin, with the head filed flat.

Modern flush-sided coaches can be made on a perspex body shell, the window openings being masked with tape before painting. This technique is at its best when an airbrush is employed.

Roofs and floors are generally made from wood although, in recent years,

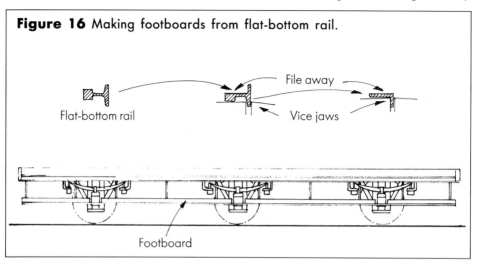

Figure 16 Making footboards from flat-bottom rail.

Flat-bottom rail

File away

Vice jaws

Footboard

there is a growing tendency to make the roofs from moulded plastic sheet.

Although the bogie coach only came into use in Britain in the 1890s, its spread was quite rapid, with the result that, by 1910, most main-line trains were made up of this pattern of vehicle. From the modeller's viewpoint, this is a very good thing, as the bogie coach is much happier on the under-scale curves of the normal model layout. However, four-wheeled coaches are also perfectly happy on reasonable curves and, if one wishes to move back in time, then this type of stock will be needed.

The six-wheeled coach is a beast on the model and wasn't all that wonderful in full-sized practice either. However, this was more due to irregular track than to tight curves, the six-wheeled coach being a very hard-riding vehicle. On the model, the problem is persuading it to negotiate corners.

Where curves are very easy it is possible to give the centre axle sufficient sideplay to enable the coach to negotiate

them. A more sophisticated approach is the Clemenson system. Here the outer axles are carried in pivoting frames linked to a sliding central assembly. Given good workmanship, this arrangement certainly delivers the goods. Happily, etched brass six-wheeled stock is frequently provided with this form of underframe and, with careful assembly, a good running coach capable of taking curves of around 600mm radius can be built. There is another way round this problem: the centre wheels can be either flangeless, or, better still, fixed in their axleboxes and have flats filed on their bottoms. In both cases we have a long wheelbase four-wheeled coach masquerading as a six-wheeler. The deception is made easier because six-wheeled coaches were almost always provided with full length footboards, and this helps to hide the wheels.

Most coaches before 1900 were built with footboards and the practice continued into the twentieth century. It arose because, although raised platforms

came into use in the earliest days of
British railways, many smaller stations
did not have them raised very far off the
rail level, and a little assistance in climb-
ing aboard was needed, hence the footboards and long grab handles beside the
doors.

On four- and six-wheeled coaches
there is little difficulty fitting footboards.
On bogie stock we hit a snag, for prototype bogies only move a few degrees
off the straight so the footboards were
normally continuous. Standard model
practice is to divide them into three
units, mounting the outer ends on the
bogies themselves.

Footboards can be made from thin
wood, card, styrene sheet or metal. Personally I prefer the latter — it is not only
stronger, but the boards can also be
soldered to wire supports and tack
soldered to axleboxes. Folding footboards from thin sheet is not easy, commercial angle section is costly, but with a
very little work, excellent 4mm scale
footboards can be made from code 100
flat-bottom rail. The process is set out in
Figure 16; note that one side of the head
is filed away before turning the angle

over and filing both head and flange flat.

Before I leave coaches, I should mention two types of associated vehicle. The
first is the full van. This is normally built
as part of a batch of coaches, to a similar
profile and on similar underframes.
However, vans have roughly twice the
life of their sibling coaches and so one
finds, at the time of writing, that on a
train of MkIII stock in the latest InterCity
livery, the van is an uprated MkI of early
1950s design! The vans also included
specialized postal coaches and in addition one might meet bullion vans, the
last of which were built by BR just after
the Great Train Robbery.

The second type of vehicle is the
passenger-rated goods vehicle. These
were generally four-wheeled stock, but
were not only painted in passenger colours and provided with vacuum brakes,
but also had different suspension and,
not infrequently, were fitted with the
large diameter solid wheel used on
coaches rather than the smaller spoked
wagon wheel. The main categories were
horse boxes, carriage vans, vans for
perishable goods such as meat, and milk
vans.

CHAPTER 14
Passenger traffic

Superficially, passenger traffic is much the same as it has always been, the main difference being the increase in multiple unit working which, whilst highly efficient, removes a lot of variety from the operating pattern. In addition there have been many losses, not the least of which are the secondary and branch line trains and the once extensive network of through coaches. Another type of service which has also gone is the special coach, though this began to wither around the turn of the century as the size of coaches increased to the point where it was no longer possible to provide a special vehicle for a family excursion.

The most obvious difference between the steam age passenger train and its modern diesel or electrically powered equivalent is that in the steam age the power unit was almost always at the front of the train. This meant that, wherever a service terminated, it was necessary to get a locomotive on the other end of the train. Although the same condition applied to a freight train, the need to re-marshal the wagons meant that the turn-around was automatic.

There were three main methods of reversal: run-round loops, spare locomotives and station pilots. The run-round allowed the same locomotive to work the train, and was clearly more suited to the comparatively leisurely workings of a feeder branch than to an intensive main-line service, since, at best, it took a good 10 minutes to carry out. After the train arrived, the coaches were detached and, if need be, backed into the loop. The locomotive would then run forward, the points would be reversed and the locomotive would pass the coaches on the loop road, running onto the main line and then, after a further point reversal, back onto the coaches. Whilst this was being done, it was not too much trouble to detach or attach vans or horse boxes, as well as any through coaches that might have been attached to the two to four coaches used for the service.

Where a more rapid turn-round was required, the normal practice was to provide a loco spur at the end of the terminal road where a spare locomotive would wait, invariably a tank rather than a tender engine. When the train arrived, the original train engine would be uncoupled and the spare run onto the other end, coupled up and, in due course, given the right of way. After the train had left, the original train engine, now the spare, backed into the loop.

This arrangement is clearly at its best where the train service is frequent. In model terms it was rarely used in the early days of the hobby simply because it required a very large loco stud, but nowadays this is no longer a serious difficulty; indeed, if anything, the main problem is knowing how best to make use of the large stud owned by most enthusiasts.

The third arrangement, involving either the station pilot or the carriage shunter, was strictly for long-distance trains hauled by large tender locomotives. Here the train arrives in the terminal road and the train engine is detached. A shunter now couples on the

Two local trains on Geoff Bigmore's O gauge 'Bigston to Archway' garden railway. On the high level we have a train of North London four-wheeled coaches headed by a North London four-wheeled coaches headed by a North London 4–4–0T whilst below an LNER 'N2' 0–6–2T hauls a quad-art suburban set on the main line.

LNER 'V2' Class No 4771 Green Arrow heads a rake of Pullman coaches out of Bigston station on Geoff Bigmore's layout.

rear and draws the empty coaches clear, releasing the express locomotive which proceeds to the loco depot for turning, fuelling and watering. The shunter then

i)   pushes the coaches back into the same platform or
ii) pushes the coaches into the departure platform or
iii) takes the coaches to the carriage sidings to be cleaned and have their lavatory tanks refilled.

Which option is chosen depends very much on the precise operational requirements of the train in question, and all three methods have been used at a single station.

Unlike local services, which generally ran with a fixed rake of coaches, in quite a few cases semi-permanently coupled with special shortened buffing gear, main-line trains were frequently reformed. Often a train was split at a major junction, each part taking a different route. A variation on this theme was the slip coach, which was in the steam age a highly spectacular way of providing a local service from a non-stop express. It can be carried out on the model, but really requires some form of magnetic retarder to slow the slip coach down and allow it to stop in the platform. On the prototype, slip workings were only carried out where there was a station pilot to hand to pull the coach into the platform should the guard in charge misjudge the drop.

Slip coaches, and most through coaches, were brake composite vehicles, having first, third and luggage sections and, before 1900, second class accommodation as well. Even on a late 64 ft long coach, this left precious little room in any section and so, in many cases, a through portion comprised two

or more coaches.

It was not wholly unusual for a restaurant car to be detached from a train part of the way through its run. This was more frequent in the early days of restaurant services for the simple reason that a limited number of coaches had to serve as many trains as possible and there was little reason to haul the coach and its crew further than it need go, especially if lunch had already been served to all who needed it, and the journey would end before afternoon tea could be completed. Sleeping coaches were also only added to overnight services, only a few of the longer-distance sleepers forming complete trains.

On the model, a basic four-car rake can be transformed by adding one extra coach, a sleeping car, restaurant or buffet car or a mail coach. This is not strictly in accordance with full-sized practice, but it allows a better variety of services where there is insufficient space to provide storage for a number of different set trains.

I must make one point very clear, which is that there are few reliable records of train formations. A number of diagrams do exist but, apart from the major expresses which were often made up from special coaches built to produce a de luxe train, there was no pressure on the staff to maintain a fixed formation. Coaches did break down, and the function of the wheel tapper, or, to use his correct title, the carriage and wagon inspector, was to check on the condition of every coach that passed through his station, and he had the absolute power to order a defective vehicle to be taken off the train there and then.

One reason failures in service were, and still are, fairly uncommon is that coaches were overhauled on a regular

A down Southend train approaching Barking in 1951, headed by an LMS-built 4–4–2 'Tilbury Tank'. Note the mixture of stock in a standard suburban rake; the leading coach is an LMS standard non-corridor brake third, followed by a low-roofed Midland coach. A pair of close-coupled coaches with brake end follow and then yet another brake compartment. This heterogeneous collection of vehicles is typical of many steam-age trains.

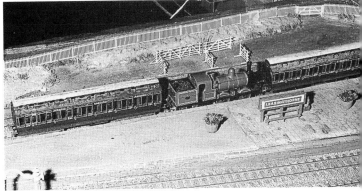

Push-pull working, North Eastern style: a Fletcher BTP (Bogie Tank, Passenger) 0–4–4 well tank sandwiched between a pair of non-corridor clerestory coaches converted for push-pull working.

basis. Of course, the ideal arrangement is to replace a complete train, and wherever possible this was done, but from time to time a single vehicle would reach the point for overhaul before its companions and, once again, the set was reformed. As a result, many steam age trains consisted of a collection of stock of different designs and periods, and the all too common model practice of having the rake of uniform pattern is not strictly in accord with what actually took place on the railway.

Before I leave the arrangement of coaches, I must mention the push-pull or auto-coach. This was either an old coach which had been converted or, as in the case of the GWR, a special-purpose vehicle which was provided with equipment which allowed a driver in a compartment at the back end of the train to have limited control over the locomotive. Various methods were in vogue; the GWR favoured a simple but cumbersome system of rods beneath the coaches which operated the regulator through levers. Most other railways used air or vacuum pipes to work servo-motors.

The push-pull train is an excellent way of working a local service on the model, as there is no need to provide run-round facilities at its terminal bays and it is perfectly feasible to run the branch under an overbridge or into a tunnel and just stop it there. As the mainstay of the layout it does, however, lack interest, but salvation is at hand. Push-pull services often hauled vans, horse boxes and, above all, through coaches, and the locomotives were often detached to do a little shunting. This was less common on the GWR, as its system was rather more difficult to take apart and con-

siderably more difficult to join together than the pneumatic systems favoured by other lines.

Passenger trains were rarely without some form of merchandise traffic, and the vans were not there solely to carry passengers' luggage. Some trains had a high proportion of such vans and in certain cases, such as the newspaper and mail trains, it was the passengers who were there on sufferance. In addition, a fair amount of important traffic was carried in vans hooked onto the rear of local services; these could be horse boxes, milk vans (or later, tank wagons), meat and even fish.

In addition, most main lines and many secondary routes had so much parcels traffic that complete van trains were run at passenger speeds. In addition, a highly perishable freight, such as fruit, meat and fish, would often be worked at passenger speeds.

A variegated range of coaching stock and vans in Nottingham Castle station on Norman Eagles' 0 gauge LMS 'Sherwood Section' system. Note the two central carriage sidings in the station and the train of vans on the far side.

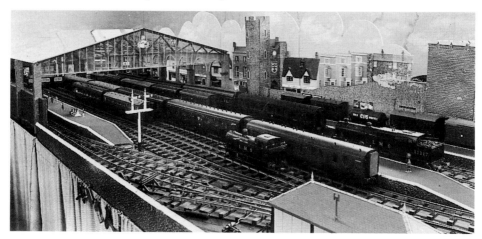

CHAPTER 15
Electric incursions

Although we are dealing with steam traction, it has to be pointed out that electric and internal combustion traction has been used on railways in Britain for over a century. This short chapter is provided to complete the prototype picture, but is not in any way intended to suggest that non-steam traction ought to be included on a steam age model. Indeed, it is my opinion that if one really wants to model an electrified railway, it is best to look overseas for the prototype.

Electric traction began with the Volks Electric Railway in Brighton as early as 1883; the line is still running, although nothing but the route remains of the original system, which was initially two-rail traction. Apart from the City and South London tube, the main developments took place after 1900. The initial surge lost momentum after the First World War on all but the Southern and London Underground lines. There were virtually no loco-hauled electric services in Britain, the exceptions being the NER Newport–Shildon freight-only scheme, the Metropolitan Railway passenger services from Baker Street, initially to Harrow but mainly to Rickmansworth, where steam traction took over, and the District Line Southend trains as far as

Barking. In the final years, there was the Manchester–Sheffield electrification through Woodhead tunnel, but although the 25kv AC electric locomotives were initially worked alongside steam services, their purpose was to replace the older system.

The extensive Southern three-rail network, the scattered lines owned by the LMS, the LNER Tyneside lines and, below all, the London Underground were mainly three- or four-rail multiple unit services. Apart from certain Southern routes, they were local suburban lines providing commuter services. The exceptions were the Midland's experimental overhead route to Heysham, which was a prototype for an unfulfilled dream of main-line electric working, and the later Manchester South Junction & Altrincham line, which again was a test-bed for the 1500V DC main-line electrification proposed in the 1930s. If one discounts its interest in London Transport routes, the GWR had no electrification on its system.

I said earlier that the Southern had some main-line routes. These were, however, not only run as if they were outer suburban services, but on one occasion Maunsell, the CME, referred to

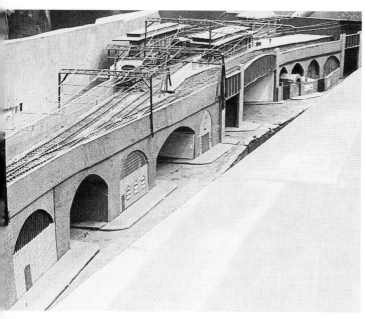

the new Portsmouth route as only a suburban run. His comments have been borne out, and all SR main-line services are, today, extensively used by commuters.

Way back in the 1930s it was customary to include a Southern electric set on the layout *to excuse the third rail*. Today, it is necessary to add a dummy third rail to the model to account for the presence of multiple unit stock. It is pleasing to report that not only are a growing number of modellers favouring the Southern, but many are going to the trouble of adding a third rail to the main line and platform bays to allow the addition of an electrified local service. This, I feel, is the only area where alternative traction can sensibly impinge upon the steam scene; indeed, unless one is modelling the extremities, the post-1935 Southern scene is incomplete without its electric stock. The LMS and LNER elec-

trified lines were so restricted that it is a trifle difficult to justify a third rail.

Internal combustion railcars were first introduced, with somewhat disappointing results, in the early 1900s, but it was not until the GWR developed its streamlined railcar fleet in the mid '30s that diesel traction came onto the main lines. Contrary to popular belief, the main function of the railcars was not to serve sleepy country branches, but to operate lightly loaded local services over main lines. As the fleet only amounted to some 38 cars, including the two parcels vans, they can hardly be regarded as a major part of the GW scene. The British Railways diesel units did, however, make considerable inroads into local services in the last years of steam, and no post-1955 scene would be complete without at least one such set.

Diesel shunters were mainly used by the LMS, but once again, even after the war, there were very few of them. The GWR and Southern owned a couple, the LNER only added them after the outbreak of war. However, internal combustion was far more common on private lines; the North Sunderland Railway even went so far as to operate the first regular standard gauge diesel-hauled passenger trains in Britain, with a diminutive four-wheeled diesel mechanical locomotive. The Ford Motor Company had two very impressive Bo-Bo diesel electric shunters in their extensive private railway system at Dagenham, but the main industrial diesel shunter was a simple four- or six-coupled mechanically driven beast. Furthermore, the first oil-engined shunters cannot possibly be called diesels — they were built before Dr Diesel developed his dead-end system of air injection which has somehow become the generic name for the compression-ignition engine. In point of fact, the first British oil-engined locomotives used the Ackroyd-Stuart engine which is the true progenitor of the modern compression-ignition engine.

There are, at the time of writing, versions of the later GWR railcars and some early BR DMUs available ready to run in 4mm scale, together with kits for BR DMUs and both Southern and London Transport electric stock. There are also kits for some of the older industrial diesel locomotives, so there is the possibility of adding these variations to the model, but in the main the early electric and diesel prototypes are a highly specialized field for the modelmaker on the lookout for something totally different, who is prepared not only to delve into reference books for the necessary information, but is also ready to scratchbuild a fair proportion of his models.

CHAPTER 16
Wagons galore

Although the loss of the steam locomotives is the most obvious point of difference, the major change between the steam age and the diesel era on Britain's railways has been the wholesale abandonment of local goods traffic and the disappearance of a wonderful array of specialist and general-purpose wagons. The sheer variety offered by the goods wagon and the operating interest it can bring to a layout is the most endearing facet of the steam age railway, and since so much of this one-time familiar part of the railway scene has been lost and forgotten, I will be dealing with it in considerable detail over the next few chapters.

The standard four-wheeled British goods wagon, which saw out the steam age, came into being, albeit in a slightly smaller version, around 1835. Initially of 8 ton capacity, it went up first to 10 tons and then to 12 tons, uprated to 13 tons during the Second World War. It had three, five, seven or nine planks, side doors, occasionally end doors and, even more rarely, bottom doors as well. The latter were mainly provided for coal traffic, of which more later.

As the 10 ton wagon was common by 1890, and the 12 ton saw service around the turn of the century, the standard ready-to-run commercial wagon can be used for the initial wagon fleet on almost any steam age railway. However, this is only a stop-gap policy, since each company insisted on doing things differently. There were considerable differences in detail, and minor changes in length. The nearest thing to a standard open wagon was the Railway Clearing House (RCH) standard for privately owned vehicles, which, whilst not supported by law, was effective.

Box vans were rather more individual. Initially the framing was outside, but before long some companies decided to have it inside and leave the exterior smooth. Then roof profiles differed, as did heights, widths and, above all, the way doors were hung or arranged to slide. Vans for perishable traffic were provided with vents; these were more important in the ends than in the sides, since the flow of air through the vehicle when the train was in motion had a decided cooling effect (the wind chill factor was fully appreciated even at the dawn of the railway age).

The British four-wheeled wagon had a short wheelbase, normally 10 ft, occasionally 12 ft, rarely longer. The vehicle was usually 16 ft to 18 ft long and 8 ft in width, and would be fitted with hand-operated brakes. Prior to 1900, these might well be on one side only, but eventually the Board of Trade insisted that the brakes must be capable of being applied on either side, though not necessarily released from both. In the main, the Morton-pattern lever brake, with a cam action to allow the levers to apply the brakes with a downward thrust, was employed. However, the GWR, which made a fetish of being different, used an ingenious ratchet brake which could be applied on one side and released on the other. The Board of Trade did not like it, but the GWR persisted in fitting it well into the '20s.

I've mentioned fitted goods vehicles in the coach section, but I must also point out that, as time went on, more and more goods vehicles were either 'fitted', that is to say provided with vacuum brakes, or 'piped', merely provided with a vacuum pipe allowing the vehicle to be put into a fitted train. However, unlike the passenger-rated vehicles, these wagons were not suited for really high speeds, but as no one booked a fitted freight much above 50 mph until British Railways days, it wasn't too obvious that, at high speeds, the traditional short wheelbase goods wagon could bounce itself off the track! This led to the rapid disappearance of the traditional goods wagon, and with it much of the

A rake of private owner wagons are seen here beyond Geoff Bigmore's 'J39' 0-6-0 No 2706. The wagons were common visitors in the London district, though one, black with a single B on the doors, is in the freelance livery of 'Bigmore's Best Coal'.

A plastic kit for a GWR 'Iron Mink' supplied as a pre-painted Great Northern gunpowder van. This is a sound commercial ploy, for the older gunpowder vans were close copies of the standard GW vehicle. Iron construction was favoured since with wooden stock gunpowder got into the grain of the wood, producing a highly flammable vehicle, needing only a spark to precipitate a catastrophe.

specialized traffic railways once enjoyed, but as this only began at the very end of steam traction, it is mentioned only to explain why current goods vehicles have a longer wheelbase.

The short, loose-coupled goods wagon, which limited trains to speeds of around 30 mph, was criticized for the last 100 years of its life but obstinately remained in use because its virtues outweighed its snags. For a start, most goods-handling facilities were designed around a 16 ft long vehicle. Indeed, the wagon turntable, the last examples of which were installed in the 1950s, necessitated a short vehicle. In addition, numerous tipplers were also based

around the standard wagon. It remains an abiding mystery why, instead of using the hopper wagon, which could discharge its load into a suitable chute, the majority of British railways preferred instead to up-end or invert the entire vehicle. After all, the hopper wagon was around when the first steam locomotives made their hesitant steps, and the old North Eastern Railway made extensive use of this type of wagon for mineral traffic.

Equally important, but with the exception of mineral traffic, there was little call for large wagons. Although a busy rail-linked factory might send out a score or more filled wagons each day, the probability was that each wagon would end up in a different place. There were nonetheless attempts to promote larger wagons. The Caledonian introduced a 20 ton bogie coal wagon, but it had little impact. The GWR later introduced a four-wheeled 20 ton steel coal wagon with better success; it used this vehicle for its own loco coal and persuaded a number of large collieries to adopt it as well. A useful discount on tonnage rates helped. Another notable high-capacity wagon was the bogie brick wagon introduced by the LNER in the 1930s for a specific traffic.

Although each company had its own wagon stock, and goods trains in its territory would have a high proportion of the owning company's wagons, through traffic ensured that foreign vehicles would appear in the train. There were in addition the private owner wagons, which were mainly used for coal and other mineral traffic.

In theory, when a wagon owned by Company A arrived in the yard of Company X and was unloaded, it was promptly returned empty to its owner. In practice, if the staff of Company X had a load waiting and someone else's wagon to hand, they just piled it in and sent the wagon off to Company M. After a few such moves, Company A started to send round notes to the effect of 'Please can we have our wagon back?' In addition, staff in goods yards were none too keen to return their own company's wagons to the proper place; if there was spare siding room, they tended to hang on to them in case they had a need for them later in the month.

To keep track of where wagons went,

An impressive train of 4mm scale NER coal hoppers at Leasingthorne. A kit is available for this wagon, making the construction of trains of this nature merely a matter of steady application.

and to apportion revenue between the companies, the Railway Clearing House was established. It had men at all junctions whose job was to note the passing of wagons, a wonderful job for a trainspotter had the practice not disappeared about the time trainspotting became organized. To assist in locating wagons, the better organized companies codified the vehicles, the best-known system being that of the GWR, which provided every vehicle type with a code name and broke the groups down by a suffix letter. This was initially a telegraphic code, for throughout the latter half of the nineteenth century the business of all industrialized countries was conducted by telegraph. It was an excellent system because, unlike the telephone, it did not interrupt the recipient and, also unlike the telephone, both parties had a written record. In addition, unlike the telephone, one thought first and sent the message afterwards. It is possible, nay probable, that Fax and Electronic Mail may restore this civilized system.

However, the cost of sending a telegram put a premium on brevity, so the practice of using mutually agreed codes arose. Clearly, it was easier to ask for a MINK than a box van, particularly as the precise type of vehicle could be determined by a single letter suffix. With a few exceptions (the open wagon was unimaginatively termed OPEN) the names were taken, apparently at random, from a zoological dictionary. The next step, a logical one, was to paint the code name on the wagon.

Today, we do have a good selection of ready-to-run goods vehicles for the steam age, and whilst the pre-group modeller is not directly catered for, suitable transfers are available to enable near matches to be rebranded. However, the more serious steam-age modeller will soon turn to kits. The basic vehicles, open and box vans, and the commoner specials, such as cattle and tank wagons, are covered by plastic kits. Whilst a few of the earlier 4mm scale kits were rather rough and ready, the majority today are of good quality and relatively easy to assemble.

The more specialized types of wagon are catered for by etched brass kits. Once again, some of the earlier models were poor and were provided with instruction which, for the less experienced modeller, were more hindrance than help. There has been a very distinct improvement here.

Scratchbuilding wagons is not unduly difficult, particularly as one can frequently use a commercial underframe, thus getting round the trickiest part of the job, aligning the axleboxes. In view of the enormous variety of goods wagons that existed in the steam age, a little judicious scratchbuilding is quite rewarding. The utilitarian nature of the prototype makes it largely a matter of fitting four detailed sides to a simple rectangular floor and, if necessary, adding a roof. Very few tools are needed, and so it is a very popular theme for demonstration stands at model railway exhibitions. I would advise any reader who wants to try scratchbuilding to locate a demonstrator at a local show and ask his advice.

Left *Typical of modern ready-to-run 4mm scale stock, these three wagons are colourfully finished in private liveries. In each case the vehicles are authentic, but only the oil tank would have been seen very far off a regular route before 1940. The hopper wagon on the far right was a fairly rare beast before 1950, and would be confined to a regular working between a mine and the plant.*

Right *An example of a good etched brass kit for a 4mm scale model, a well thought out set of parts coupled with a set of instructions containing scale drawings and livery details. Building such a model is pure pleasure.*

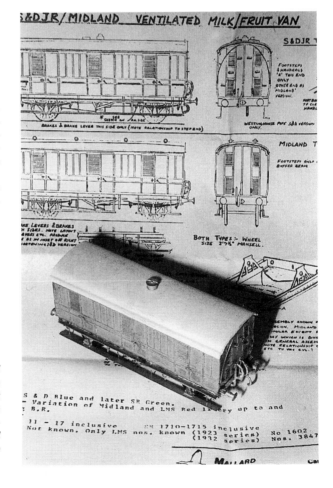

Above *Coal was the mainstay of the steam-age railway and, in the middle years, nowhere was this more significant than in the North East, where the railway system originated around a scattered group of early colliery lines. 'Leasingthorne', a 4mm scale layout based on turn-of-the-century NER practice, was a fine exhibition model where mineral traffic took pride of place. Here we see a train of NER hopper wagons headed by a NER 0–6–0 trundling steadily through the station.*

Below *The colliery at Leasingthorne. This shows how, in 4mm scale, it is possible to give the impression of a full set of colliery workings in a space hardly large enough for a scale-sized pithead complex.*

CHAPTER 17
Coal and other minerals

It is one thing to build or buy a collection of variegated goods wagons, but it is another thing to use them correctly. I shall, in the next few chapters, deal with the basics of freight operation, both on the prototype and how it can be simulated on the model. Where better to start than with the mineral that began the railway story, coal.

Coal

It might seem superfluous to mention that the steam age in Britain was synonymous with coal, but on the other hand it is all too easy to forget that, until the 1960s, most of our energy needs were met by this indigenous fuel. Throughout the Victorian and Edwardian period much of industry was powered by steam, which meant that coal-fired boilers were needed. As a boy I was fascinated by the steam cranes and other steam-powered equipment found around construction sites, and if these were not coal-fired, they were most certainly fuelled by coke. More to the point, homes were heated by coal and, until the 1920s, most were indirectly lit, through the gas mains, by the same material. Towns with only 4 to 5,000 inhabitants often had their own gasworks,

and it was not until the spread of the National Grid in the '30s that electricity became widely available.

Coal was needed in quantity. This was no problem, and it is largely why the railways were built. Much as we like to think of the express passenger train as the epitome of the railway, the simple fact is that, apart from the final decade of the steam age, it was the coal train that paid for the system. Forget the thundering 'Kings' on the glamorous West Country expresses — it was the long trains of Welsh coal headed by Churchward's 2-8-0s that kept the GWR solvent. However, for most of the steam age the standard coal train was a rake of loose-coupled wagons headed by one or two rugged, simple 0-6-0s. The wagons hardly changed, a simple wooden box on four wheels, though the load went up steadily from 8 tons gross to 13 tons, with 16 and 20 ton steel wagons coming in towards the end.

At any station with a decent goods yard, one siding was almost exclusively set over to coal traffic. Adjacent to this track would be the coal bins for storage, not infrequently made from old sleepers. They might lie alongside the track, the most obvious place, or be on

Gretley Colliery on Norman Eagles' layout was even more cramped, but this is the way with all 7mm scale models. Despite this, the essence of the prototype was brought out and the traffic working could be accurately simulated despite the very abbreviated facilities.

the far side of the yard. The reason for this was that domestic coal, by tonnage the largest part of the coal merchant's business, went out in 1 cwt sacks. To fill one, the coal was first shovelled into a special weighing machine which had, at the top, a large chute. The weighing mechanism was designed to trip suddenly at a predetermined load, and when this happened the coal was tipped into the sack and loaded onto the cart. When the cart was full, two men would set off to sell it, while another might spend some time shovelling coal into the wheelbarrow and filling one of the bins for later use.

Coal for industrial users would be loaded into a cart, and again this was most easily done if the tail of the cart could be run up alongside the wagon. The station weighbridge was used to determine the quantity delivered and entered on the invoice.

It was common practice for coal mer-

chants to keep a lot of their stock in the wagons, only unloading on demand. As the railway companies objected to having their precious fleet tied up unprofitably, they charged demurrage on wagons detained over a reasonable period (their term, not the coal merchants'), hence the willingness of many merchants to purchase their own wagons. Most private owner wagons were owned by collieries or coal merchants, and were invariably reserved for coal traffic — one trip and the insides were filthy.

The North Eastern Railway, which inherited the early coal railways, made a practice of employing coal drops which sometimes exploited the lie of the land, but were more commonly constructed on earth banks with brickwork coal cells. The principle was simple: the wagons were provided with bottom doors and, when positioned above the requisite cell, a pin was removed, the

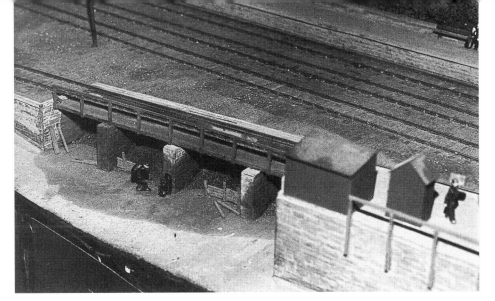

Above *A close up view of a typical set of coal drops in 4mm scale. Note how the coal piles are secured with removable poling boards. Two filled coal sacks rest against a central supporting pillar. Here the tracks are at ground level and the road drops down, a very effective arrangement for a front-of-baseboard set-up.*

Below *The North Eastern Railway preferred coal drops, and where the lie of the land did not make it easy to arrange for a low-level road access, they constructed ramps to lift the hopper and bottom door wagons clear of the working area. This arrangement is best for a rear-of-baseboard location, as shown here. This photograph also shows a weighbridge, close to the coal drops, whilst in the foreground a dray is being loaded with beer in barrels, which have been unloaded onto the raised ramp from the van. This is typical of the attention to authentic detail that characterized 'Leasingthorne'.*

doors dropped and most of the coal fell out. The last few hundredweight had to be shovelled out manually, except where a hopper-pattern wagon was used. The NER had plenty of these, and a few large box-like wagons with hopper interiors. Of course, where the layout was suitable, other lines used coal drops, but unlike the NER rarely, if ever, went to the trouble of constructing ramps for this purpose. Wagons with bottom doors were frequently distinguished by a white 'V' on the side opposite the drop doors.

Although we speak of coal as a single entity, in practice the quality varied according to the mine from which it came and the seam from which it was mined. Most people are, I fancy, aware that there was steam coal and anthracite, but in my youth the merchants offered a much wider selection than this with several pence differential between the best and worst coals. The various grades were separated in different bins. I can't recall any case of the bins being prominently marked; in most cases the workmen not only knew which bin was which, but were able to recognize the various grades.

Industrial users with rail connections frequently got their coal in by the wagonload. In most cases it was simply offloaded into the bunker by hand, but where large quantities were involved and it was not convenient to use bottom discharge, the wagons were up-ended. There are two ways of doing this: to turn the entire wagon over, or to up-end it over the chute. For this latter system end doors were required, and for any wagon so fitted, and a very high proportion were, the practice was to paint a diagonal white band across the wagon with the high end alongside the door.

End tipplers were very popular around docks, where the wagons were emptied into seagoing or coastal colliers.

At power stations and other inland users of bulk coal, the rotary wagon tippler was frequently used, but gasworks and ironworks were more likely to lift individual wagons to a high level and drop the coal directly into the retorts. In the smaller installations, the coal was trans-shipped into narrow gauge tipping wagons, and these were frequently manhandled to their ultimate destination.

Modelling coal

Quite apart from its importance in the steam age, coal has another fascination for the modeller. Of all the minerals that are carried by rail, it is far and away the easiest to model. At least, it used to be, for of recent years a small difficulty has arisen — the raw material is a trifle hard to obtain in the small quantities we need.

In other words, the ideal material for modelling coal is coal! Forget the rather unrealistic plastic pellets sold by model shops, the real thing is best. Coal has a delightful characteristic — it is extremely friable and is easily broken down into tiny fragments. My method is to wrap a lump in a piece of rag, then take it out onto a stone step and hammer it into submission. One or two lumps provide all the coal you're likely to need for a lifetime's modelling. As I said, the only snag is that it is rather difficult to get hold of a single knob of coal, but you can usually scrounge a couple of lumps, either at the coal yard or at a preservation site.

Modern gooey adhesives stick it down adequately. You can, if you wish, build up a complete heap of coal, but the usual procedure is to carve a block of softboard or wood into the rough shape of the pile, then glue the scale-sized coal to that.

Wagon loads are best built up on a sheet of stout card or thin ply raised on a block of wood. In this way the load can be easily tilted down and removed between running sessions so that the loaded wagons can depart empty.

Model coal sacks are available, and probably well worth buying. They can also be made from putty; I would recommend two-part epoxy putty or a modelling compound such as Das for this.

Other minerals

Although coal was the mainstay of the steam age railway's mineral traffic, and indeed remains, albeit in a different form, an important part of British Rail's freight business, many other minerals were rail borne. By and large, they were handled in much the same fashion as was bulk coal; wagons were loaded at the quarry or mine, transported to their destination and there unloaded by mechanical means. Once again, if the end user was small, men were employed

Most minerals were loaded into open wagons from over-track hoppers of varied design. It is generally possible to make these load loose material into model wagons, and many commercial loading devices have been marketed. This photo shows a scratchbuilt version, which has the added advantage of being highly visual and an excellent feature for an exhibition layout.

to dig the stuff out. This would happen when, for example, a single wagonload of ballast was sent to a small station for building or road works. In such cases, where the usage was occasional, it would clearly be uneconomic to provide expensive handling facilities.

The method of manual unloading was simple enough. A cart or, in later years, a lorry would be backed up against the side of the wagon, with its tailgate already dropped. The side door of the wagon would then be dropped and, if there were top doors as well, these would be opened to make it easier to move the material forward. After that, it was just a matter of sheer back-breaking shovel work to move the mineral forward into the road vehicle. This is where the traditional two-wheeled horse-drawn cart scored heavily, since no fancy equipment was needed to tip the load onto the ground at its destination — you got two men to hold down the shafts whilst the horse was drawn clear, then the tailgate was dropped and cart up-ended. A motor lorry needed a tippler gear fitted at extra expense.

However, most modellers prefer to concentrate on the other end of the business, a quarry being a very popular way of dealing with a corner, with a single siding going into a rough hole in the landscaping.

This arrangement is highly improbable. The more usual arrangement was to use light narrow gauge tracks inside the quarry and trans-ship the mineral to the lineside. There it was either tipped directly into the standard gauge wagons, which were generally at a lower level, or emptied into bunkers from which the rail wagons were loaded. Other methods of trans-shipment were belt conveyers and overhead ropeways.

There are obvious benefits to be gained from adopting these more prototypical approaches to loading minerals, and each offers a modelling challenge. The narrow gauge feeder is more easily arranged in 4mm and 7mm scales, though a few model belt conveyers have been produced. So far as I know, overhead ropeways, in model form, are confined to passenger-carrying cars, and the production of one for mineral use would be an interesting challenge to the keen modelmaker.

Slate

One very important mineral required special treatment, and that was slate. I don't propose to go into it in tremendous detail for one simple reason — it was extremely localized, being concentrated in North Wales. Furthermore, there are a number of excellent books on the narrow gauge slate lines which provide ample information for anyone wishing to model this traffic, though here the impulse generally begins with a desire to model a narrow gauge railway and ends up with the conclusion that it had best carry slate.

In model form, slate can be made from thin styrene sheet, but, as with coal, we have a very friable material which can, with care, be split into very thin sheets and then, painstakingly, cut into scale-sized rectangles. Once again, we have the problem of obtaining the raw material, for slate roofs are becoming rare.

CHAPTER 18
Agricultural merchandise

Agricultural traffic formed an important and diverse part of the railway's freight traffic. The three main divisions, dairy products, livestock and vegetables, required distinctly different approaches and were tackled with different types of vehicle.

Milk

The most urgent traffic was undoubtedly milk, for it was vital to get the supplies from the farms to the towns and cities as rapidly as possible so that the user had a chance of getting it before it went sour. Initially, the traffic was carried in churns, iron kegs that were designed to be as large as practicable. The traditional churn was a tall conical container which when tilted, so that one side was vertical, could be rolled along a reasonably flat surface by one man even when full of milk. The later squat churn, the type used today, hardly came into regular railway use, but that is getting ahead of the story.

The short life of unrefrigerated milk meant it had to travel at passenger speeds, often as part of a local train. Small quantities could be carried in the normal vans, but it was rapidly realized that, at the 40 to 50 miles an hour that

the trains travelled, there was a wonderful opportunity to keep the product fresh with a good stiff blast of air. Special

We must never forget where milk originates; a small herd on the Macclesfield club's OO gauge exhibition layout.

The six-wheeled GWR Siphons are well known and often found on branch models, but the older four-wheeled versions, which are far happier on tight model curves, are sadly neglected. Here we see an example on Frank Colson's 4mm scale layout of the late '40s.

milk vans were introduced, all with ample ventilation. The most thorough-going approach came from the GWR, with the ubiquitous Siphon van. Initially four-wheeled, these distinctive vehicles, with their slatted sides, were lengthened first to six wheels and finally to large bogie stock. These last reverted to solid sides and ample louvre ventilators, but the principle of a good stiff draught remained throughout the life of the milk van.

The milk was brought to the station by cart and manhandled onto the platform to await the arrival of the milk train. This was generally the first passenger service of the day, and without doubt the slowest, since not only did it stop at every station on its route, but each stop was long enough to allow the perspiring staff to roll the heavy churns onto the waiting vans. As the train ran into the town, churns might well be offloaded for the local dairies, but in general the vans were steadily filled and, in due course, arrived at a major rail centre.

Here they would be marshalled into a complete milk train which would then set off for the main centre of population. Until the turn of the century, and before the advent of true mixed traffic machines, old passenger locomotives would be employed on such duties. E. L. Ahrons in his classic account of railway operation in the 1880s and 1890s had a good deal to say about GWR workings into Paddington, which were often tackled by 7 ft 2-2-2s, mostly of the 'Sir Alexander' Class, lovely machines until autumn leaves got onto the rails. By 1910, however, 2-6-0 mixed traffic locomotives were available for such duties.

By the '30s a different approach was taken after milk factories were set up in the country to pasteurize and chill the milk, separate the cream, make butter and cheese and generally provide the reliable, hygienic product we tend nowadays to take for granted. These factories were situated alongside the main line and, instead of decanting the pasteurized milk into churns, piped it directly into glass-lined tank wagons which were then marshalled into trains, as were the old vans, and then sent directly to the large cities for bottling and distribution.

This is a very important point to keep in mind. For a start, no post-war model should have milk churns, and only the odd immediate pre-war branch might still have milk collected in this primitive fashion. Certainly you cannot logically mix milk churns and milk tankers on a single layout. Furthermore, whilst I have no firm evidence of the exact usage, the switch to the squat, cylindrical churn took place at roughly the same time as rail traffic changed from churn to tanker. Therefore, as a general rule, the cylindrical churn should be associated with the milk factory rather than the railway proper.

Milk tanks were hooked onto the rear of passenger trains, but the fact that a busy factory could fill eight or more each day led to them being collected by the milk specials. On arrival, the milk

train would be rapidly unloaded and the product taken to the plants to be put into the familiar bottles before delivery to the doorstep. At least, by 1930 this was the general practice.

Before this, we had the milk float which consisted of a small two-wheeled cart which held a large churn, beautifully embellished with polished brass strips. The milkman would drive this along the street, calling loudly as he went. The housewife, or in the more well-to-do suburbs, the cook general, would then emerge carrying a quart jug which would be filled with foaming milk from a properly certified dipper which was stamped by the local Weights and Measures inspector as being a true pint, half pint or whatever. As the recipient often received a quantity of foam in her measure, the milkman did rather nicely, thank you.

In addition to milk there is, of course, cheese and butter, not to mention cream. Having lived for many years in Devon, I often feel that unless the spoon

Most milk tank wagons on model layouts are six-wheeled, but the initial examples, depicted in these excellent 7mm scale models by Geoff Bigmore, ran on a shorter four-wheeled chassis and are more suited to the sharper curves of the model.

actually stands upright in the jar, it isn't really cream, but that's by the way. I want to talk about butter. In my childhood, it arrived in large boxes, and was doled out by the dairyman. This was a fascinating sight as the butter was scooped out and dropped onto a marble slab, running with cold water. A skilful worker could get a good half ounce of water into the final half pound of butter.

However, we're getting a little off the rails. Butter travelled in wooden boxes, lined with several layers of greaseproof paper. In wealthier districts, an astute dairyman would have his supply sent direct from a farm, where it was produced in the old-fashioned way. It didn't really taste any better or do you any more good, but it certainly cost the odd penny a pound more, which proved, if proof were needed, that it was a superior product!

Livestock and meat

One of the more confusing traits of the English language is its ability to alter the meaning of words. Once upon a time,

butchers were to be found in a shambles, but just as we no longer associate a shambles with a killing ground, so we have largely lost the strict usage of butcher who was literally the man who killed as a matter of course. Properly speaking, a butcher's shop has a slaughterhouse at the back whence cattle, sheep and pigs were driven on the hoof and slaughtered more or less on demand. This, before the advent of fast transportation and, later, refrigeration, was the only way the customer could get fresh meat. The initial impact of the rail network was to save the beasts a long and tiring trek. Instead of being herded for weeks to the town, they would be driven from the farm to the station and there loaded into special wagons, taken to town and thence to the slaughterhouse.

The cattle wagon was a secure van, roofed to keep the rain off, with ample air space above to enable the animals to breathe freely and with slats and holes in the base to allow the inevitable mess to be hosed out afterwards. Until the last few years of cattle transit it was the custom to coat the inside with fresh lime-wash at the end of each journey. The practice was discontinued when it was realized that it might promote foot rot. I suspect the reason it took so long for this to be discovered was that the overwhelming majority of the beasts that were taken by train were slaughtered long before any ill effects of the journey could be detected.

The final type of cattle wagon built by British Railways was based closely on the GWR design, which came into being around the turn of the century. It was noteworthy for one important feature, the movable partition that, at a stroke, eliminated the need to provide short, medium and long cattle trucks to cater for different levels of demand. Whilst this appears fairly simple, in point of fact it needed a very secure locking mechanism, for the principle of cattle movement by train was simple — the

beasts were loaded crosswise and as many as would fit into the length were pushed inside. This remains the only economical way known of preventing them falling over each other in transit.

As the small slaughterhouse was replaced by the centralized abattoir, largely as public squeamishness grew and demanded that animals should be killed out of sight of the population, more and more butchers obtained their meat ready killed. At about the same time, a very important technological development took place. Refrigeration became a practical proposition.

Prior to this, ice was a precious commodity outside midwinter. Large estates had ice houses, underground chambers with thick walls where ice, cut from the lake, was stored in straw in the hope that, in midsummer, enough would remain to allow the Family to enjoy chilled drinks and desserts. Although the first refrigerating plants were large and

Above left *Cattle wagons headed by a GWR 0–6–0 saddle tank. Note the lime-wash on the lower planks.*

Right *A 7mm scale model of a Midland Railway large cattle wagon. Note once again the liberal use of limewash.*

Leasingthorne was not exclusively mineral, and here we have a rake of three cattle wagons heading a short and very mixed train — the two open wagons are carrying pit props.

cumbersome, it became possible not only to build large cold chambers, but in addition ice could be made all the year round.

This enabled the railways to introduce chilled vans for the safe transit of meat. Initially, these were grossly inefficient; the idea was not so much to produce a well-insulated box, but rather to increase the chilling effect created by the van's passage through the atmosphere at anything up to 50 miles an hour by passing the air over large blocks of ice. That the ice was melted on arrival was quite immaterial. It was not until later that the concept of a double-skinned van, with the interstices packed with insulation, came into being. These vans, however, were not intended so much for moving home-grown meat as for transporting the frozen carcasses imported on the new refrigerated ships from the Antipodes. As speed was of the essence, the vans were passenger rated and fitted with vacuum brakes.

Cattle traffic was important in the steam age. Indeed, such was its value that when Ashburton fair was held, and the railway was called upon to send several cattle trains out of the small terminus in a few hours, the passenger trains terminated at Buckfastleigh and a Western National bus completed the journey.

Produce

Although refrigeration was well established in the Victorian era, it was not until the last years of steam that deep-freezing of vegetables became commercially viable. As a result, a large proportion of farm produce was the subject of seasonal traffic. In point of fact, this was precisely the sort of traffic that a railway can handle effectively, if not necessarily economically. The prime requirement was a large number of clean open wagons, ample siding space and a little forward planning to ensure that, as soon as the crop was ready, the wagons were there waiting to be loaded. If need be, the coal siding would be cleared for the occasion. The fun got fast and furious when several farms wanted to use the same facilities at the same time! This is a type of traffic that is rarely featured on a model, though it would not be overly difficult to set up a broccoli special as an occasional feature. You would simply need a good supply of standard open wagons which would be brought in at the beginning of the day's working and taken out, loaded, at the end.

Some crops — potatoes are a prime example — can be stored for a considerable time after harvesting, so these were sent out in dribs and drabs, loaded into sacks and stowed in open wagons. Grain and flour were also sacked loads. The wagons would be loaded with the sacks stowed vertically and, if the total load did not exceed the wagon's limit, a further 14 sacks could be laid horizontally on top. However, as grain and flour is ruined by rain and bagged potatoes are not exactly improved, it was customary to cover open wagons loaded with these and other perishable commodities with sheets, large tarpaulins which had the owning company's initials stencilled upon them.

More delicate produce such as lettuces and tomatoes was sent to market in flat boxes, initially timber but, towards the end of steam, cardboard. Often such merchandise went in vans, whilst flowers, normally a high value and very perishable commodity, were almost always sent by van. Fruit was also dispatched in boxes, and here special ventilated vans were provided to keep the produce cool and fresh during the journey.

Farm removal

Now and then a farmer would sell his land and move, lock, stock and barrel, to another district. This was hardly a regular traffic for the railway, but when it did happen the publicity department generally went to town; British Railways even went so far as to produce a documentary film covering just such a shift. The resulting train was quite a collection of vans, cattle wagons and implement wagons, complete with one passenger coach for the farmer, his family and those of his staff who were joining in the move. Although it was a very impressive sight, it was nowhere near so difficult to organize as the publicity handouts suggested. In point of fact, it was almost certainly easier to collect the necessary vehicles on the spot for a preplanned special than to rustle up an extra cattle truck to deal with the unexpected load one market day.

Horse boxes

Cattle wagons were all very well for most breeds, but horses called for special treatment. Largely, this was because most traffic in horses involved thoroughbred beasts, either for racing or hunting, and so, instead of being expected to travel crushed up together, each horse had a lush padded stall in which to travel. Indeed, the horse box was a most luxurious vehicle all round. Most horse boxes would take two animals, and also had a compartment at one end for the groom or even the owner. Horse boxes were normally coupled to the rear of passenger trains, though for major race meetings special trains would often be put on.

CHAPTER 19
General freight traffic

During the steam age, the railway was a common carrier by law, which meant that it had to accept anything offered, and take it to anywhere there was a station. However, there was no compulsion to charge a uniform rate and so the infamous rate book came into being. In theory it quoted a charge for every category of goods, though on occasions a prospective customer managed to produce something that didn't quite fit. There was a long and involved joke about this, the punch line being 'Rabbits is 'ares and rats is dogs, but this 'ere tortoise is an h'insect so it goes free!'

Fortunately, this is a complication that doesn't impinge on the model; indeed,

as most general merchandise was loaded out of sight in the goods shed, the whole process can be carried out in the imagination. Loading and unloading was a matter of manhandling, aided considerably by the simple principle that most common loads were packaged in one hundredweight (approximately 100 kg) units, the practical limit for one man to lift. Larger packages called for the use of a crane. All but the smallest goods depots had one, and on occasions there were two, though this was not always obvious since the second was inside the goods shed. Except in the very large depots, these were manually operated; the steam age yard was a labour inten-

sive system, for the simple reason that manpower is extremely flexible and remarkably effective.

Some types of merchandise occasionally required distinctive vehicles.

Building materials

During the steam age, many builders' merchants had their premises alongside the railway in order to cut down on the amount of trans-shipment involved. As they ordered supplies in bulk, these came in full wagon loads and were generally offloaded fairly quickly and put into store. Frequently, one firm would combine the function of coal merchant and builders' supplier.

The main builders' traffic is shown in the table below. Timber, cement, plaster and lime were invariably stored under cover, while the more durable materials were often stored in the open. In addition to these raw materials, there would be a wide selection of finished goods, baths, toilet fittings, doors, window frames and other furniture. Whilst this type of traffic did not call for special purpose vehicles, the items are quite noticeable and make for interesting special loads for open wagons.

Oil

Although at first sight oil traffic only made a serious impact in the twentieth century, we must not forget that this not only covers the main modelling period but that oil, for lubrication and illumination, was carried from the earliest days. Indeed, one of the more horrific of early railway accidents, the collision at Abergele in 1868, would have been relatively insignificant had not the runaway wagons that caused the disaster been carrying kerosene in barrels.

Almost to the end of our period a large amount of rail-borne oil traffic was carried in barrels, initially casks, but during the popular modelling periods it would have been taken around in the familar large steel drums. Petrol was initially carried in rectangular 2 gallon cans; these were the original method of fuelling cars before the advent of the petrol pump proper, which did not come into general use until the 1920s. Similar cans were also used to supply paraffin and kerosene.

The oil tank wagon made a tentative appearance around 1900, but did not become common until between the wars. It is interesting that until the '50s

Left This shot across the goods sidings on Ken Payne's 'Castle Coombe' EM gauge layout shows the typical mix of wagons seen in a steam-age station. Two bogie bolster wagons, used for transporting long loads, generally timber baulks or steel girders, are to the fore, whilst, in the right foreground we have a glimpse of a steam traction engine loaded on an implement wagon.

Merchandise	Vehicle
Sand and ballast	Normal open wagons
Cement, lime, plaster[1]	Vans or sheeted wagons
Timber	Open wagons or timber wagons
Bricks	Open wagons[2]
Slates, tiles	Open wagons
Pipes	Open wagons

[1] These were delivered in 1 and $\frac{1}{2}$ cwt bags
[2] The LNER had some high-capacity bogie wagons for this traffic

Three wagons on a small quayside siding in 3mm scale (TT gauge). From left to right we have a sheeted open wagon, the tarpaulin branded for the Great Eastern Railway, a standard small oil tank, privately owned, whilst the open wagon is in early LNER livery. The small coastal sailing barge is in keeping with the size of the quay.

the major oil companies used rail to transport bulk supplies from the refineries to their main depots, a practice that has continued to this day where pipelines do not exist. From the mid-'30s onwards, special unloading facilities were provided where trains of tankers could discharge their contents, via standpipes, into storage tanks.

Beer

Even in Victorian times, when independent local breweries abounded, beer was a regular load. Some lines even went so far as to build special ale wagons, though most were happy to load the barrels into open wagons. There was just one small snag about this – it was all too easy for an enterprising train crew to stop along some quiet section of line and tap a cask. As a result, by the turn of the century it became more and more the case that beer was sent in vans. The GWR even went so far as to convert a number of cattle wagons into ale vans.

The steel beer cask is only compatible with the very end of steam power, and for most of our period the standard beer

barrel was the norm. The bowed profile, whilst pleasing to the eye, had a far more practical purpose – it made the heavy cask easier to roll from place to place.

A few beer tankers did exist, and these were glass-lined tanks identical to the familiar milk tank wagon. However, one would need to be very certain before introducing one on a layout. It wasn't so much that there was no demand for such large supplies — quite the contrary — but during the steam age only bottling plants were equipped to cope with bulk supplies. The normal pub was only capable of handling bulk beer in barrels.

Containers

Although containerization was used extensively during the canal era, the idea failed to carry over onto the railways and it was not until the 1930s, when a good deal of traffic had been lost to road transport, that a belated attempt was made to encourage the use of these convenient devices.

The steam age container was a much smaller unit than the modern ISO container, and fitted neatly onto a four-wheeled flat truck. Whilst designs varied in detail, the general principle was a wood or metal crate with side or end doors and provided with four lifting loops so it could be easily swung up off the open wagon by crane and deposited on a flat lorry.

The container is very much associated in the public mind with furniture removal, mainly because this particular aspect was widely promoted to the general public. However, the main use was in providing a convenient means of despatching large quantities of manufactured goods from a factory to a wholesaler. It was very attractive where high-value items were involved, since the container could be locked and sealed before leaving the works, greatly reducing the possibility of pilferage *en route*. Some containers were ventilated for meat traffic and, as with much such traffic, a proportion were privately owned.

There was one very interesting and distinctive container running on the LMS in the '30s. It was a relatively small tank which was sent empty from London to Glasgow to be filled with water.

The owners were a firm of whisky blenders who made a point of using Loch Katrine water for this purpose. However, as one of the partners was W. S. Norris, a keen modeller who, at that time, preferred the GWR, the tank was painted in GW coach livery.

Special wagons

Whilst the standard open wagon and van took care of the majority of general traffic, there were a large number of special-purpose vehicles to handle the exceptions.

Probably the most common were the bolster wagons. These usually comprised a pair of short flat wagons, semi-permanently coupled together and each with a pivoting bolster mounted centrally. These could carry long timbers or tree trunks, and were often coupled to a low flat match truck to allow the load to project beyond the end of a wagon. In addition, long bogie bolster wagons were built to take longer timbers with ease. This type of wagon was also used for carrying steel sections, though steel plates were generally carried on strongly

Another selection of mixed freight wagons of the steam age. A typical van is immediately behind the loco, followed by a PO open with a rectangular tar tank behind. A gunpowder wagon is alongside the small hut built to contain the blasting powder used in the nearby quarries.

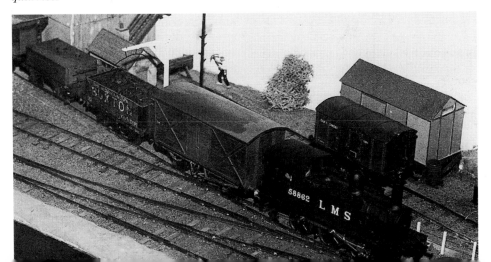

built long-wheelbase wagons.

Another fairly common type of special-purpose wagon was the low-loading implement wagon. Its main duty was to take traction engines, road rollers and portable engines around the country and, in the last days of steam, performed the same duties for bulldozers and other forms of earth-moving machinery. It was rather more substantial than the flat carriage truck which dated back to the early days of railway travel, when the upper classes had their private coaches hitched on the rear of the train so that they could continue their journey in comfort after arriving at the nearest station to their destination.

The heavier crocodile bogie wagon was less common; it was intended for very large items indeed and was rarely seen off the main line. These and other special-purpose wagons for major loads make interesting models but require a good deal of ingenuity to justify their presence on the model. There was, for example, the propeller wagon, a stoutly constructed vehicle with a strong steel trestle to which a ship's propeller could be lashed. As many propellers went outside the loading gauge, their transit called for complex and expensive arrangements, and thus this traffic rapidly shifted to the road. One advantage from the consignee's viewpoint was that such loads can travel on the road at any time whereas on the railway they were strictly Sundays only.

Fortunately, there is now a large number of excellent books covering the wagon stock of the major companies, well illustrated and, in most cases, lavishly supplied with drawings, often to 4mm scale. These describe innumerable special-purpose wagons, but whilst many provide a wonderful challenge for a modelmaker, I would sound a note of caution. Check the number of wagons built to that and associated designs. Then check the numbers of standard open and box wagons and from these figures work out the odds of seeing one such special vehicle. Until my eighteenth birthday I lived in houses backing on to railways, and spent hours watching trains. Yet I can't recall ever seeing a well wagon, the most common special-purpose vehicle, until I went to work in the London docks.

Brake vans

Last of all, since this is undoubtedly its proper place, we come to the brake van. Unlike present-day freight trains, where the guard rides in the locomotive, for the entire steam age he rode in a special van at the end of the train. When, as was usually the case, a high proportion, if not all, of the wagons in the train were unbraked and loose coupled, the guard had a busy time keeping the couplings taut by judicious use of his handbrake. He also supplemented the engine's brake power when needed, a complex code of signals on the locomotive's whistle controlling the use.

The brake van was definitely not a common user vehicle and in many cases was branded with its home depot. It rarely strayed off its own metals, and then only over lines where running powers were in force. More importantly, it matched the locomotive in front — an LMS engine pulled a goods train ending in an LMS brake van. The major exception to this rule concerned the Cheshire Lines Committee, a joint LMS–LNER line which had no locomotives but possessed its own freight stock and goods brakes, which were generally hauled by LNER locomotives.

CHAPTER 20
Handling the freight

Perhaps the most significant difference between the pattern of freight working in the steam age and current British Rail practice is that whereas modern freight trains are block workings, the old system broke up and reformed goods trains at frequent intervals. This was implicit in the network of small stations serving their immediate neighbourhood.

Let us take the case of a consignment of cabbages offered at an intermediate station on a small rural branch line. It makes up a full wagon load, which simplifies matters for everyone, and into the bargain there is a suitable five-plank wagon in the siding. As soon as it is loaded, the porter puts a label on it indicating its ultimate destination. It then waits until the arrival of the local goods train.

Rainham station in the early '50s with a fairly typical array of goods wagons in the sidings. It is not so much that standard open wagons and box vans predominate — there is simply a marked absence of anything else!

Manhandling a wagon at Alton Towers. This loaded box van has been moved from the goods shed by sheer muscle power.

One point needs to be made here. Shunting did not take place continuously at a local goods yard, as it would be highly dangerous. If a wagon needed to be moved during the working day, muscle power was needed. This is where the railway horse came into its own, for it could easily drag the odd wagon around the sidings. In the absence of a horse, manpower could be used; two or possibly three men could get a wagon rolling, and once this was done, one could keep it moving. One man, using a pinch bar, could do it single-handed, but it took time.

The local, or pick-up, goods train ran slowly along the line calling at each station. Wagons would be put down and

picked up, and taken, in the case of a branch, to the junction. Frequently, the pick-up goods would then proceed along the main line to pick up and drop further wagons, but if this were inconvenient it would simply terminate at the junction and the locomotive would then be used to sort the wagons into separate cuts to go on main line goods trains to a variety of destinations. With any luck, our wagon of cabbages would now be picked up by a goods train that was heading directly to its intended destination.

Things didn't always work out this way, and the majority of wagons went to a marshalling yard. This might be a very large array of loops fed from a ramp, allowing the wagons to run through by gravity. Unfortunately, spectacular though it may be, a hump yard doesn't work all that well in model form and, worse still, it is rather less fun to operate than the smaller, simpler flat marshalling yard where the trains are moved about by locomotive power.

The general principle of the flat marshalling yard was to have a couple of reception roads, where the incoming trains stood whilst waiting for attention, and then as many sorting roads as were needed to handle the traffic for each destination. Each train was taken by the shunting locomotive and the wagons were then run into the appropriate sidings. However, as the trains may have needed to be split later in their journey, every effort was made to keep vehicles for the same destination together. A shorter spur road was provided for brake vans and a water crane was provided to replenish the shunting locomotive's tanks as necessary. Such yards were often termed concentration yards.

Large conurbations would have several such yards, frequently a legacy of the many pre-grouping companies that served the area, and wagons were moved between these yards on trip workings. In extreme cases, a wagon might spend a whole day being shunted around a large city, ending up a little more than a mile from its point of origin before it could be put on the train that would take it a hundred miles or more to its ultimate destination.

The process sounds extremely inefficient and, to a large extent, it was. Attempts were made to overcome the worst of the faults, but were overtaken by events and, above all, the flexibility of road transport. However, when it comes to operation of a model railway, the features that hamstrung the prototype enhance the model. One of the most attractive parts of steam age model railway operation is the simulation of goods working.

In its most elementary form, in a simple goods yard, shunting can provide hours of fun. This is exemplified by the small shunting yard which was first described over 60 years ago by A.R. Walkley, whose HO scale folding yard was the first published example of what is, today, a common exhibition feature.

The model consists of three sidings, a shunting spur and a small loco shed, embellished scenically to taste. Automatic couplings are essential; Walkley's model incorporated a home-made version of the present tension lock coupling, the *de facto* standard for British ready-to-run models. Indeed, the layout could be produced in its entirety from standard commercial equipment.

In its simplest form, each wagon must be distinctive in design and colouring, and there must be enough wagons to occupy two thirds of the siding space clear of the uncoupling ramps. The shunting spur must be restricted in length — no great problem there! Finally, there must be a card for each wagon — something of the size of a visiting card is about right.

The pack is shuffled and, assuming the spur takes four wagons plus the locomotive, the top four cards are exposed and laid down in order. The operator then assembles those four wagons, in that order, into a train. If the spur takes three or five, then the number of exposed cards will, of course, corres-

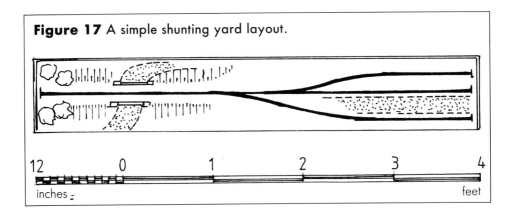

Figure 17 A simple shunting yard layout.

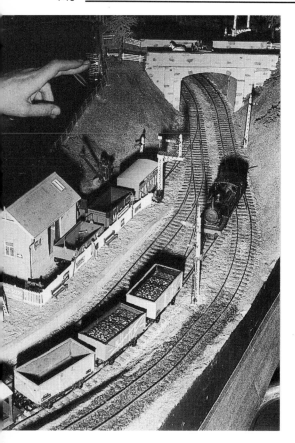

pond. It sounds very simple, but it has baffled professional railwaymen, used to having a much longer shunting spur, for the sorting has to be carefully planned if one is not to get the whole thing hopelessly jammed.

This is, of course, very elementary shunting. If one is setting out to simulate the freight working of the prototype on a realistic layout, a little more sophistication is required. A lot depends on the type of layout involved; clearly, the simple branch terminus to fiddle yard model cannot exhibit the complexities of a complete system, so the ideal starting point is the small terminus.

An incoming goods train will have its locomotive at the front end. The first step is to run the locomotive round the train and hook it onto the back alongside the brake van so that it can shunt the train. It will, of course, contain a selection of different wagons carrying the various goods consigned to the station, and the next thing to do is to get these alongside their normal unloading positions. This is made a trifle difficult if, as is usually the case, a wagon is there already, so the first step is to remove the freshly loaded and empty wagons.

The loaded wagons present no problem — they will form the next freight train to leave the station. A common practice is to detach the brake van and place it either at the end of the departure road or, if as is usually the case on a small model, this refinement is missing, on the run-round loop. The loaded wagons can then be assembled in front of it to form the next train. It is clear that whilst the goods wagons are being sorted out, the capacity of the sidings will be fully extended, so in all probability there will also be wagons alongside the platform face. These would need to be moved clear should a passenger train be scheduled, adding to the number of shunting movements.

The empty wagons provide a problem — does the stationmaster, in his capacity as yardmaster, send them away, or should he hang on to them in case an unexpected load arrives? The answer depends first on the capacity of the station and the number of new wagons awaiting unloading, second on the nature of the wagon itself and last, but most important of all, on the stationmaster's knowledge of the traffic pattern of the district and his experience as a railwayman. Clearly, there is little point in hoarding a large number of standard open wagons, as these arrive daily for unloading. Van traffic will also be fairly predictable, so most, if not all, of the empties can be returned with thanks. The more specialized vehicles are more of a problem.

Where there is a steady one-way traffic in, for example, live cattle leaving the market for the city abattoirs, arrangements will exist for empty stock to be delivered to the station. The problem arises with the less frequent traffic. Let's take two separate types of traffic as examples.

Large sheets of plate glass were sent in special wagons with central trestles and means of securing the delicate load securely and safely. If a new row of shops was being built, then such a wagon would arrive with a consignment for the local builder. Once safely unloaded, the station staff would heave a sigh of relief and send the wagon back whence

it came since there was no possibility that a return load would ever eventuate.

Road rollers are very slow moving vehicles, so it is standard practice to load them onto something else if they have to travel more than a few miles between jobs. When, in the steam age, one of the local roads needed repair, a roller would arrive on an implement wagon and be offloaded at the end-loading dock. Clearly, in anything from a few days to a month or more, the roller is going to be sent somewhere else. The stationmaster would, if possible, hang on to the implement wagon to make life easier, but there would be two snags. The first would be not having a little-used spur where the wagon could lurk for a couple of weeks, and the second would be receiving a request for its immediate return since it was needed elsewhere.

This business of demand for wagons can be simulated on a model, but for the time being we'll continue with the simple sorting out of our train. Each newly

Above left *Shunting in progress at Cheviotdale. Even a small, simple layout provides ample operating scope if the goods sidings are laid out to permit interesting working.*

Right *The goods facilities at Alton Towers were relatively simple; the goods shed was a simple structure with a massive canopy covering the loading area. A standard box van has just been filled.*

arrived wagon now has to be located at or near its unloading point. A lot of quiet amusement can be provided simply by having an important spur facing the other way from the rest of the sidings, thus involving an extra run-round, which can be a little troublesome should the run-round loop be occupied, as it probably will be. All in all, the model operator can spend a good 15 minutes' actual time sorting out a goods train and getting ready to send a new one back along the branch.

When the train enters the fiddle yard, it is a good idea to take every wagon off the rails and replace it with a fresh one, otherwise we arrive at the ridiculous arrangement where apparently those idiots at the junction persist in returning our vehicles! At the very least, loads must be removed and replaced. In the home this can be done at any convenient moment, although at an exhibition it

is not desirable to do so in view of the public, at least not during running sessions. In a number of well-planned exhibition lines, the physical unloading is carried out under cover inside goods sheds and factories whose backs are open to the operator, but obviously hidden from the viewer. The whole business of loading and unloading goods wagons can be great fun, and this point is appreciated by the major model train manufacturers who produce loading and unloading devices. Although tied in with a toylike approach, we should never lose sight of the fact that the same arrangement, suitably developed on a well-designed model railway, adds enormously to the operating interest of the model.

Where the layout has more than one station, or to be more precise, set of goods sidings, additional refinements can be introduced, whilst on a complete system quite a high degree of operating interest can be achieved easily by simple colour coding. This is feasible since a large proportion of prototype goods traffic involved full wagon-loads being transferred from one specific point on the network to another.

The principle is that each destination has a set colour and each wagon normally has at least two corresponding colour spots on its solebar, denoting the two points between which it shuttles. Each operator can then determine quickly whether a wagon is intended for him or not. Wagons can have three or even four spots, whilst an unmarked wagon would be a wild card and could be unloaded at any appropriate station. Although this does fix the wagon's routes, it is not too inconvenient in practice.

An alternative to this is to drill small holes into which coloured map pins can

be inserted. This would denote the destination point of each wagon in a train, but would not confine any wagon to a fixed route; however, it means that at the start of each session all wagons need to be marked and, furthermore, on arrival at their destinations they need to be re-coded. There are ways of dealing with this, but before I go into them, another method of ordering wagon routes needs to be considered.

It has one tremendous advantage in that it closely follows prototype practice, since each wagon gets a waybill giving its load and ultimate destination. On the prototype, a special clip or housing is provided for documentation but clearly, even in the largest model scale, this is out of the question. What we can do is to have a record card corresponding to each wagon (see Figure 18).

All cards are cut to a uniform size for

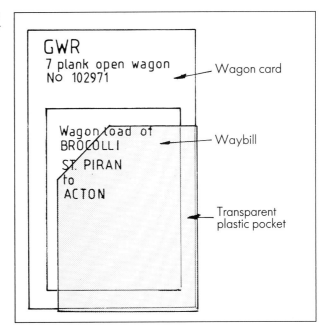

Above left *The goods shed at Archway station on Geoff Bigmore's O gauge layout.*

Figure 18 Wagon card and waybill.

This hand-worked yard crane once stood at Colyton station, now the terminus of the Seaton Tramway.

convenience and a full description of the wagon, including its running number, is written or typed on the card. A pocket is provided for the waybill, generally made by sticking a piece of thin transparent plastic to the card with adhesive tape. In practice the description is quite compact, since one clearly follows the prototype practice, quoting the official name and its unique running number. This is where it makes good sense to renumber ready-to-run wagons that are duplicated.

The waybills are made out for a specific load to go to a specific point. This is normally done well in advance and, obviously, the waybills, like the cards, are standardized. They are then dealt out to the individual stations, and the operator must then match load to wagon.

This is where the fun begins. Whilst the more common traffic, which fits nicely into a standard open wagon or un-fitted van, presents few problems, since there are usually plenty around, anything calling for a special vehicle means that one has to be dispatched to the station. This means that it has to be worked empty stock from wherever it is, thus simulating a common prototype problem.

The operator first matches waybills to wagons, then assembles the wagons into the train. He then collects all the wagon cards together and hands them to the next operator who first sorts through them to see which wagons are for his station, removes these wagons, adds any he has loaded and, having removed the appropriate cards and replaced them with any he has added, sends the train on its way and hands the cards to the next man down the line.

It is normal to provide a series of pockets along the baseboard edge to hold not only the cards for the next train, but also the cards for the wagons already in the station. These could be further broken down into empty and loaded wagons, whilst a number of pockets could be provided for the loaded wagons to cope with different destinations on the imaginary system. These do not need to exist in reality, and all one needs is a scheduled service which, whilst ending in a fiddle yard, is deemed to go to some specific point in Britain.

This is, of course, a very simplified

description of what is usually a highly sophisticated arrangement. Much of the interest in this system lies in two areas — devising imaginary loads for the wagons and, from this, determining their correct destinations and allocating these loads to a particular working session.

The first is a long process which, thankfully, does not need to be done at once and can be carried out away from the layout. It has many pleasant side effects, one of which is suggesting possible new wagons to be added to the collection. The second is capable of a number of arrangements, all of which require the introduction of a chance factor. However, completely random choice is not always a good idea, since it can all too easily produce a totally un-balanced set of waybills. A lot can be gleaned from wargaming, where complex rules govern the possible outcome of any move by a player.

The random element is best governed by ancient methods. The first is the stack of cards, or in this case, waybills which are shuffled and the requisite number dealt out. The second is that the random selection of numbers is governed by casting a die. Reverting to the example of wargamers, they have 8-, 12- and 20-sided dice so a visit to a specialist games shop could be a very useful step.

In its simplest form, the die is cast to determine the number of loads on offer, then the requisite number of waybills are drawn. This can, however, produce some weird, indeed impossible, per-

Loading general merchandise into a waiting van. Normally, such work would be carried out inside the goods shed, but it was not unheard of for this to be done in the open when pressure of traffic made it necessary.

mutations and so the selection needs monitoring. One possibility is to determine a block load, possibly throwing dice to determine how many coal wagons are needed, and then dealing with other staple traffic in a like manner. Then further throws will determine not only the nature of the special loads, but also whether, on this occasion, there will be any such loads at all.

Going further, the preparation of waybills to some generalized overall plan is the sort of job a simple home computer can take in its stride, given a suitable piece of software. Unfortunately, this would need to be specially written for the layout. A complex generator capable of creating a core program to suit any layout is perfectly feasible, but the snag is that it has very little commercial value at present since, unlike a normal computer game or a standard application program, it is not likely to sell many copies. On the credit side, this project does not involve any electronic interfaces, nor does it demand that the computer is in the railway room, since it would be perfectly acceptable for the entire schedule to take the form of a printout which would then be used to moderate the basic timetable.

I have not gone into any great detail as to the exact way the card and waybill system is worked for one very simple reason — I have had the pleasure of operating a number of layouts using such a system, and all differed in detail, all had been developed over a period of time and all were equally interesting to use. It is not so much that there are no rules, as clearly the main object must always be to simulate, as closely as possible, the traffic pattern of the old steam age railway. This does need tailoring to the precise arrangements of the model so each case must, to a considerable extent, be individual. The method of introducing a random element and the means of moderating this factor to avoid inconsistencies are open to change as one's experience grows. Hence it is not so much a case of adhering to an established principle, but of developing a workable system for one's own layout by trial and error.

Apart from the added realism a traffic management system adds to operation, it has a side advantage for the development of the layout itself. The more one studies prototype traffic arrangements, the more one comes across interesting services which call out to be represented on the model. Bit by bit one adds facilities to the model in order to cope with the developing traffic pattern. I have frequently seen on established layouts which are operated in this fashion, additional sidings, new goods depots and other features which have been put there solely to provide a reason for running a particular type of wagon. This is an exact reproduction of prototype development and gives an added reason for running the model in this fashion. It improves the realism of the layout in more ways than one.

CHAPTER 21
Beyond the fence

A full-sized railway does not exist in a vacuum, so to create the impression of reality we need to imply that our stations serve an appropriate community. How far one goes with this depends on your own preferences. Indeed, there is a very real danger that an admirable principle can be so overdone that the railway becomes lost in a welter of non-railway models, and it is difficult to be sure if the end product deserves to be called a model railway at all. There is nothing inherently wrong with this — diorama construction is a valid modelling discipline which has certain very real advantages — but the end product might well be summed up in the classic phrase 'c'est magnifique, mais ce n'est pas la gare!'

Kept to sensible proportions, a scenic setting for a layout adds an extra dimension to one's modelling activities whilst enhancing the overall scheme. However, there are many pitfalls when modelling the steam age scenic setting, for the area beyond the railway fence has, if anything, changed more in the past 30 years than the railway itself. Worse, whereas an anachronism in railway equipment is at once easier for the enthusiast to correct and difficult for the lay viewer to detect, an anachronism in the background is more likely to be spotted by the viewer. It is therefore vital for the modeller to be very circumspect when creating the supporting scene. Fortunately, the current nostalgia boom has not merely brought a large number of Heritage museums into existence, but has also led to numerous albums of old photographs being published.

Buildings

Every area in Britain has its own distinctive style of building, carefully developed over centuries and using locally available materials in an economical, effective manner. The West Country cob cottage with its thatched roof contrasts with the harsher stone-built Yorkshire houses, whilst the rolling Weald of Kent produces yet another version. The railway modeller must therefore take pains to ensure that his buildings are correct for the layout's location. So runs accepted belief.

Fortunately, it just isn't so and, to understand this, we must look at how railways were built in Britain. In many cases, the stations were located on green field sites just outside the town or city

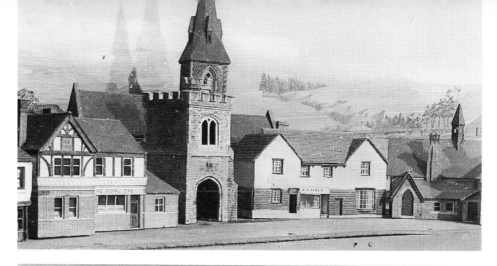

Top *A series of buildings constructed by the late Jack Nelson. The prototypes were all found in and around Barking: the central tower is all that remains of the former Barking Abbey, and the 'Royal Oak' public house alongside was situated beside the present Barking Abbey School.*

Above *More of Jack Nelson's 3.5mm scale buildings which were intended for his first HO LNWR layout.*

they served; where it was necessary to take a line through a built-up area, the poorer, run-down areas were chosen. This was partly to save expense, but also to avoid upsetting influential individuals. The 'not in my back yard' syndrome did not spring into being with the motorway — it was flourishing when the first railways were built. Agreed, there are places where the line skirts an important building — Conway Castle is a prime example — but these are rare exceptions. The engineers steered their lines away from major buildings wherever possible. Once the railway was built, it generated demand, buildings sprang up around the station and, where old buildings remained, they were soon demolished to make way for new.

Even before railways existed, local building styles were under threat. From the middle of the eighteenth century, town houses were increasingly being constructed to standardized designs found in architects' pattern books. By the time railways appeared, vernacular architecture was in decline except for the cheapest of housing. Railways accelerated this move by making standardized materials available throughout the country — slate from Wales, bricks from Lincolnshire and the London basin, wood from Scandinavia, hardware from the Black Country. From 1800 onwards, buildings are best classified not by their locality, but by their period.

Of course, there are plenty of vernacular buildings that have survived to this day, but very few of them are alongside a railway station. Not over many are even visible from the railway unless, like Durham Cathedral, they are too big to be hidden. If, for example, we take the picturesque fishing village of St Ives in Cornwall, full of quaint cottages arranged at random around a network of narrow alleyways, we discover that the station itself is surrounded by typical turn-of-the-century houses. To get rows of quaint buildings alongside our tracks calls for a good deal of modeller's licence, though one can squeeze the odd period house close to the line.

It is not too difficult to locate suitable examples of urban buildings for a steam age layout. I live in a modern house in a New Town, yet within five minutes' walk there are dozens of houses that date back to the steam age. The danger is that many have been modernized, and whilst the main structure is intact, the details have been drastically altered, the

An end-of-terrace house, typical of the buildings found alongside railways, probably dating from the mid-Victorian period. The lean-to outhouse has the air of an afterthought. This family is fortunate to have a private side access to their garden.

plain sash windows have been replaced by a double-glazed Georgian-style bow window, and the new hardwood door with its brass furniture is a far cry from the old blue-painted softwood fitting that came with the house. However, there are enough old photographs and reference books to show the standard styles of your period.

Shops can be a snare. Retail chains were rare before 1920, and were in the main confined to grocery stores. More to the point, few of the current High Street stores even existed in the steam age itself — Boots, Sainsburys, Woolworths, Burtons and Marks and Spencer are the main survivors. Grocers like Liptons and Home and Colonial were still around and, of course, it was only in the final days of steam that the supermarket made an appearance. Most small shops were run by the proprietor, whilst the chains were generally fairly small and localized. One important point to remember is that until the late '30s a distinction was made between a butcher, who killed cattle in his own slaughterhouse, and the purveyor, who bought meat from the local abattoir. Fishmongers displayed their wares on stone slabs — refrigerated displays only arrived in the '50s. There were, until the final days, few specialist radio shops, and it was not until 1950 that TV sets began to predominate. In the '30s you would usually buy your radio from the local cycle shop which often had a toy and model department as well. It was only in the centre of towns that there was sufficient business for specialization. Such present-day staples as refrigerators and washing machines were very rare indeed.

Dress shops and men's outfitters came and went, but one did not see lavish displays of lingerie until the post-war years. Departmental stores originated around the turn of the century, and while many were swallowed up by growing chains, some independents remained until the end of steam. These stores specialized in clothing, bed linen and soft furnishings, but frequently had other lines, including, in larger shops, furniture.

Trades that have vanished are corn chandlers and, to a lesser extent, ironmongers and tool shops. The ironmonger usually provided paints and decorating materials, but by 1930 the specialist decorators' supplies were appearing. This marked a general shift from having house decorating done by tradesmen towards the beginning of DIY.

Before 1930, a farrier was essential in any community, and often carried out general blacksmithing as well. As motor transport developed, these concerns took to handling repairs and sold petrol and oil, forming the origin of the garage we know today.

Farms

Whilst farmhouses were much as they are today, farming was totally different. Tractors were rare before 1939, though to say that everything was done in a 'traditional' manner begs an important question — agriculture has seen several major changes in style over the centuries.

The most important point is that although right up to 1950 a good deal of farm work was performed by animal power and was very labour intensive, steam power was adopted very early in the nineteenth century, and, latterly, the little known hot air engine provided power for various implements. Steam

A large farmhouse in 2mm scale, part of the scenic treatment on the Model Railway Club's 'Chiltern Green' layout. Note the pump beside the further ground floor window and the bulging grain sacks piled alongside the door. Presumably these are about to be manhandled into the cellar, as one of the flaps is open. Doubtless the farmhands are fetching a ladder and a length of rope — they surely can't be skiving!

ploughing was established before the turn of the century and remained in use until the 1950s, though by then the tractor was taking over. An important point to remember is that many common breeds of cattle today did not exist in any appreciable numbers in pre-war herds — a neat point, since the colouring was different.

The farm proper always had a number of cottages for the workers; these were generally built in short rows many of which can be seen from the railway, and most were built from local materials to traditional designs. In many cases, the original farmhouse was divided into dwellings when a new, more modern house was built by a prosperous farmer. Most surviving examples of these older cottages have been extensively modernized, and this can be another trap for the unwary. For most of the steam age, they were untidy working dwellings, surrounded by makeshift lean-to timber

sheds whilst the back garden would be full of vegetables, rabbit hutches and chicken sheds. Farm workers not only did not earn enough to buy very much food, they were usually too far from the shops as well.

Pubs

The most popular non-railway building must be the pub. It is rarely too large to fit comfortably into a spare corner of the layout, and there are numerous interesting designs to choose from, ranging from the traditional coaching inn to the city beer house. Whilst plenty of excellent examples from the steam age survive, few have not been extensively worked over by the brewers since the end of steam, so field research, whilst very enjoyable, can be awfully misleading. Fortunately, the inn has also been a popular subject for artists and photographers, so one can find out how a local pub looked before modernization

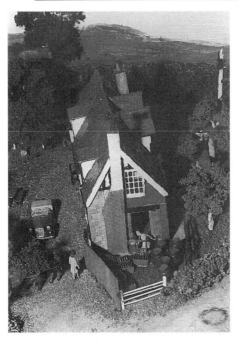

It's none too obvious from the photograph that this building is a pub, until one spots the barrels lined up ready for collection. They must be empties — no one would leave full ones outside! The model, on Martin Brent's 'Rye Harbour' is based closely on a former pub now turned into a private home.

and use this knowledge to strip the subject back to its old appearance.

Landscape

It is not necessary to say a great deal about the steam age landscape, for in broad outline it was much the same as it is today. However, as with regional buildings, it is essential to ensure that you get the appropriate type of countryside alongside your layout. I doubt if many modellers would attempt to set a

Great Eastern Railway layout in mountainous scenery, but many seem to delight in finding large outcrops of rock in the most unlikely places.

If the railway tracks occupy a large proportion of the baseboard area, and roads or buildings fill up most of the rest, there really isn't room to do more than include a few odd corners of fields and so, providing you don't go overboard on some exotic tree, you are fairly safe. Tailoring the landscape to the district modelled is of greater importance in N gauge, where it is generally easier to fit a railway into a broad expanse of countryside without making the baseboards unmanageably large.

Roads

During the Victorian period only main urban roads were paved with cobblestones and setts, while most roads were merely macadamized, that is to say over a carefully prepared foundation, small stones would be spread and compacted with a heavy roller, a surface adequate for horse-drawn traffic. Technically, the British road system remained at the level set by Turnpike Trusts during the heyday of coach travel, but in practice their condition was allowed to deteriorate for the simple reason that they received precious little use and that mainly local in nature. Roads were nothing more than feeders to the railways, and milestones and fingerposts became neglected.

The initial upswing took place in the last decade of Victoria's reign, when steam traction became more reliable and the internal combustion engine and bicycle began to provide an alternative to the train. Once motoring became reasonably reliable, the old loose road surface proved inadequate; initially the stones were bonded with tar, but later pre-mixed tarmacadam came into use. Motoring organizations started to erect road signs, but the network remained much as it had always been. The main roads of this period were between 24 ft and 30 ft in width, perfectly adequate for horse-drawn traffic where speeds tended to be fairly uniform and overtaking was the exception rather than the rule.

After 1920, road transport became more important and road markings and road signs made their appearance, but it was not until the 1930s that this was anything like universal. Although some dual carriageway roads were built between the wars, it is a simple fact that the modern motorway and expressway network only came into being after steam fell from its prime position. The modern system of road signs and extensive road markings hardly impinged on the steam age.

This certainly simplifies road con-

This street scene, on the Macclesfield club's 00 gauge layout, is typical of the 1930s. Two single decker buses are held up at the level crossing, a horse-drawn cart moves slowly along whilst the driver of the little roadster is just about to get in to drive off. No problems with parking in those days! Note the old-style road sign for the level crossing, the main bus stop, with its solidly built shelter, and the two-arm fingerpost. A bevy of Boy Scouts are heading for camp, pushing their handcart. A small detail here — one would have expected them to have come to the village to buy fresh supplies and the cart should be loaded. The phone box and pillar box complete the scene.

struction for the steam age modeller! For a start, the road widths can be kept down; 24 ft is adequate for all but major urban roads and as little as 18 ft can be used for secondary roads. A central dotted white line is all one would find, and that only by the mid-'30s. There were 'SLOW' markings and 'HALT' signs or other 'give way' indications at junctions by then, but there were not so many that their absence on the model need cause concern. The main thing to watch is that the old pattern road signs must be used; however, these are obtainable commercially.

Until 1900, horse-drawn vehicles, supplemented by the occasional steam traction engine, were the norm, and very few motor vehicles would be seen

in the closing years of the century. From 1900 to 1920 the proportion of internal combustion machines increased, but it was not until the 1920s that they became very common outside cities. Horse traction slowly died out, but railways were slow to move to internal combustion because the draught horse had other uses in the goods yards.

Steam traction on roads fought on, with a fair proportion of long-distance heavy goods being steam-hauled, but it died on the roads during the Second World War. Electric tramways, in the main an urban feature, began to lose ground to the trolleybus in the 1930s and died out in the 1950s. It is safe to say that no steam road vehicle ought to feature in a post-nationalization scene,

Left *A GWR container, hauled by a late '30s mechanical horse, rounds the bend on the Macclesfield club's layout. The occupation crossing is provided with two kissing gates to stop unwary pedestrians crossing the line without thought.*

Above right *Trams were commonplace features of the urban scene for a good part of the steam age and, in 4mm scale, there are a good many kits, including some recent plastic products that have a very wide distribution. This model, on Dick Yeo's 4mm scale urban scene, is from a cast white metal kit.*

and trams are only really compatible with the early BR liveries and not at home with either Mk1 coaches or the BR Standard classes.

One can safely assume a 20-year life for a private car of the steam age; indeed, many of those built in the middle and late '30s ran until the '60s. Lorries were shorter lived — ten years is a safer bet — though the Second World War extended the life of the late 1930s models. There were exceptions, and quite a few older motorists clung to their ageing vehicles, maintaining stoutly that 'they don't build cars like this any more!' The MOT tests only affected the very last days of our period and can be largely ignored.

There are those who say, with some justification, that one should get the right pattern feeder bus onto the station forecourt. However, there is good reason to use an inexpensive commercial model as a stop-gap and then wait for a bus fanatic to tell you what you should have done; it saves you effort and gives him a good deal of pleasure. What I don't recommend is spending a good deal of time constructing a quality kit

unless you do know it is correct for your model.

A more subtle trap lies in the horse-drawn farm vehicle. These were almost invariably built to traditional designs, the patterns being handed down through generations of wainwrights, so, for true authenticity in a rural scene, you should ensure that you get the correct type for your area. Once again, there are illustrated textbooks to hand to point you in the right direction.

While you can always find prototype justification for quite outrageous in-felicities, the scenic surround to a railway model should, surely, be there to enhance the layout. Having the appropriate road vehicles alongside the track is, I suggest, a very important part of this worthwhile objective. It can be a long-term project since, more than anything else in the scenic picture, road vehicles are easily exchanged.

Garages

The garage is a common feature of the road scene, but the present slick sites are vastly different from those of the steam age. Often, the old farriers gradually turned to servicing the newfangled machines, whilst newly built garages usually comprised a couple of large wooden sheds with a row of pumps outside, devoid of any protection from the weather. Some grotty huts at the back and the odd derelict car completed the scene.

Before 1910 there were very few pumps, and petrol and oil were sold in 2 gallon cans. The first dispensers were manually operated and used a precision piston pump worked by a rack and pinion mechanism. As electricity supplies became available, the motorized pump with an indicating dial came into use. This pump was the staple device during the last three decades of the steam age, while the now familiar self service dispensers are more in tune with the diesel era.

One important feature to remember is that even up to the last years of steam, most garages were independents, owned by a local proprietor and selling four or more brands of petrol from the forecourt, a feature only seen today on motorway service stations. The facilities were generally primitive by modern standards, only the larger stations having awnings, whilst there were plenty of fill-ing points on the main road inside towns. These were still around in the 1960s.

People

Since a railway exists to serve the community, no model railway is complete without miniature figures. Whilst these are usually the last detail to be added, they are nevertheless the touchstone that converts an arid, if technically accurate, representation into a living scene. Indeed, so far as the majority of viewers are concerned, good groupings of miniature figures will do more for the model than the most exquisite detailing of a finescale locomotive. The proper populating of a layout calls for two separate factors — a supply of suitable figures and the controlled imagination to make the most of them. In addition, it is essential to know a certain amount about fashion, and since this is easiest to cover, where better to start? It is, I feel, rather pointless to spend a great deal of time and effort ensuring that one's locomotives, coaches and wagons are correct for a chosen timescale and then casually put in model figures that are obviously out of date.

Model figures are essentially static. It is therefore advisable to assemble them in-

The former Airfix figures, now sold under the Dapol label, are fine for the steam age as they were taken from a series of pre-war LMS posters depicting railwaymen about their daily work. They need painting and must have the 'paving slabs' removed before setting them in place around the layout.

Waiting for the train at Heathfield in 1949, a typical grouping on a sleepy steam-age branch line station. Most of those present, like the author, have just got off the Exe Valley train and are waiting for the connection to Newton Abbot.

to groupings that minimize this defect. One simple solution is to have small groups apparently in conversation, but it is always as well to have some figures busy about their everyday affairs, preferably with a touch of humour.

Today, a wide range of figures are available for all popular modelling scales. They fall into three rough groupings — pre-painted plastic sets of perhaps six figures, unpainted plastic figures, and cast white metal figures. The latter can, in certain circumstances, be obtained painted, at a price.

A lot of the cheaper painted sets date from the late '50s and early '60s and are compatible with a late steam age scene. The white metal figures are generally more expensive, but are frequently sold in period sets, making life just that little

easier. The unpainted plastic sets offer the best scope for the keen modelmaker, since it is fairly easy to make modifications to them before painting. The biggest range of unpainted plastic figures is provided by the German firm, Preiser. Whilst intended for HO, they can be used with effect in 4mm scale scenes, providing they are not mixed up with 4mm scale figures. Perhaps the most important aspect of the Preiser range for the period modeller is an excellent set of turn-of-the-century period figures, which, in my opinion, are the best this firm has so far produced. There are perhaps rather too many uniformed men for a purely British scene (one individual is, I swear, an Admiral of the Royal Ruritanian Navy) but the ladies are delightful, and many could have just stepped out of a Tissot painting.

Many of the Preiser figures have movable arms and are thus very readily modified. All plastic figures are capable of being carved and cut, having bits stuck on and added. The processes are described in manuals on military modelling, where modification of larger scale figures is a standard technique. Whilst the finer points of this branch of the modelmaker's craft are next door to impossible to apply on a 4mm scale figure, many basic techniques are applicable.

Skirts, capes and, to a limited extent, loose top clothes can be cut from very thin paper, stuck in position and then stiffened with a very dilute goo produced by adding small shavings of plastic to a plastic solvent. Alternatively, parts can be moulded from epoxy putty, the best for this purpose being Milliput, which is capable of being rolled out into very thin sheets.

Painting is best done with a selection of fine brushes, and a magnifying glass on an adjustable stand is almost essential to allow you to see what you are doing. I also find that a pair of permanently closed tweezers, which can be purchased from specialist modelmakers' toolshops, are extremely useful for holding the figures in comfort.

One final point — no one willingly stands with their feet encased in a paving slab. The better figures don't have this addition, and on the others it should be cut away and the figures should be firmly cemented in place, with, for added security, a fine pin driven into one foot and pushed into a hole drilled in the platform, pavement or whatever.

Endpiece — the sunlight filters through the trees alongside the railway as the horseless carriage waits for the train to pass and the crossing gates to re-open. A pleasing piece of 7mm scale scenic modelling on Richard Chown's Irish broad gauge layout.

Index